Thinking and Writing

Thinking and Writing

A Guide for College Students

Brandywine Press

ISBN: 1-881-089-41-X

1st Printing 1997

Telephone Orders: 1-800-345-1776

Printed in the United States of America

CONTENTS

Part I

THINKING AND WRITING

UP THE CREEK WITHOUT A PADDLE

If I can convince you that it is worthwhile to master the contents of this brief text, it could be one of the most important books you will ever read. Its message is blunt: Unless you learn how to write reasonably fluent English prose, your college career won't be worth your dorm rent. Conversely, learning to write better will greatly improve your chances of later success.

Consider how you came by this book. The

instructors who added it to your syllabus did so because the writing that they see every semester distresses them. Maybe you didn't care whether you upset your high school teachers, but you might want to rethink your strategy now that you are in college. Some college instructors give grades like a hanging judge with a migraine. Others are kindly, gentle people whose concern for you deserves a response. And you are responding. You have read this far. Great!

In grade school you memorized the multiplication tables; in high school you became acquainted with some of the raw facts of the American Civil War. But chances are you never learned how to write a coherent essay about those four blood-soaked years (the Civil War, not high school). If so, you are like most Americans, and most American college students. The goal of this brief paperback is to take you inside the act of composition and show you how the language works so that you can use it with confidence.

Drudgery and drill are not the answers. If they were, college students loaded down with weighty books on English composition and grammar would know how to write by the time they are sophomores. The principles and ideas offered here are based on the assumption that anyone who has been speaking a language for several years will have taken in, consciously or not, some perception of its logic, its structure, its music. The reason that you can understand any of grammar is that it brings to full clarity the knowledge that is already within you. To take a simple example: Someone who has never heard of what the language police call a misplaced modifier can still recognize that the sentence, "Little Ethel saw a turtle skipping down the street," puts the wrong creature to skipping. A thoughtful attention to words, sentences, and paragraphs amounts to a constant drawing upon that awareness within you, which is the best means of writing well.

This handbook shows you how to pay close heed to words and the ways they connect with one another. Get a feeling for this, become conscious of the knowledge that you possess from your daily listening and speaking, and you will no longer need to refer frequently to formal principles.

Doing that will require a commitment on your part, which you have every reason to make. To do well in college, you'll need verbal control over the materials you encounter in your courses, certainly the good ones. The best especially demand both thinking and writing. You'll have to do some memorizing, but the kicker is to understand the materials and effectively demonstrate that understanding on paper. Resolve to do that, and this book will meet you more than halfway. It will cut through the stuffiness of complex rules not essential for good writing.

A student, however, must want to learn; teachers cannot work magic. A decision to be more self-critical can be an important milestone in the route to improved writing. While in prison during the 1960s the Black Panther Eldridge Cleaver learned to write brilliantly. If you are imprisoned by a part-time job, take this book with you to dip into during free moments.

STARK NAKED NEVER LEARNED THE FUTURE PERFECT TENSE

You are never so naked as when you write things down for others to criticize. A critic is commenting on our background, our education, our place in the world, our being. "Stark Naked" is the name assumed by one of the acid-soaked hippies who crossed the continent in 1965 on a bus painted with Day-Glo graffiti. Its destination over the windshield simply read "Farther." The driver, Neal Cassady—the Dean Moriarty of Jack Kerouac's *On the Road*—wore a microphone slung over his head, at one point announcing that the gas pedal had turned to spaghetti. Stark Naked, who remembers nothing of these travels, later became a published author under a different name. This brief handbook intends to convey to you how Stark Naked managed, and how you can manage, to go Farther and learn to write much better than you do now.

Stark Naked was not the sort to worry about what a gerund is, or the future perfect tense. Some good writers, to be sure, have absorbed grammar and style through daily drill, perhaps at some fine traditional boarding school. They had a vocabulary for understanding and discussing problems in writing. When a teacher said, "You've used an adverb instead of an adjective," these students knew what was meant and, for the moment that such resolutions last among the very young, they would determine never to do such a thing again. If this was not your upbringing, though, you still have a promising way of becoming a strong writer, and that is by careful listening to how the English language works, the language that you have been speaking, hearing, and reading for years. The knowledge is within you, awaiting your discovery of it.

RULES ARE NOT ALWAYS LOGICAL

Custom has established rules as useful ways of getting a reader through a mass of words on paper. One such custom, for example, makes a writer capitalize the initial letter in the first word of a sentence and follow the last word with a period, question mark, or exclamation point. A circle around the first letter could have done as well as making it a capital; a slash line might be just as easy to make as a period. A rule declares that the simple past tense of the verb "reach" is "reached," while that of "run" is "ran." Spelling has its own sets of rules. Some rules established by tradition defy logic itself. By habit that contradicts reason, the words "every" and "everyone" force a verb into the singular even if more than one actor is involved: "Every woman and every man *encounters* some disappointment."

The best case for sticking to periods and capital letters, to common tenses and the peculiarities of English spellings, and even to long-established violations of logic is that they are familiar to writers and readers, do their job well, and let everybody get on to other things. A practical argument for learning conventions is that a teacher reading an endless pile of essay examinations will find it tempting to judge each by its errors in traditional grammar, punctuation, and spelling.

Some rules once in favor among formal grammarians never really took, and for that we can be grateful. Almost but not quite vanished, for example, is a pointless rule against starting a sentence with "And," "But," or "Or." A writer with a sense of the rhythm and pacing of spoken English knows that occasionally a well chosen initial "And" can keep just the right flow between the sentence and those preceding it, while a "But" can make for exactly the needed shift in theme.

Beyond rules and usage lies the more interesting terrain of writing itself, where reason looks for the clarity of a small turn in argument, while the mind's ear listens to the silent sound of written words. The reasoning and the listening, indeed, are almost the same.

Concentration and good common sense

will tell you that some constructions are wrong not because a rule-bound grammarian has declared them wrong but because they do not make sense. Take a look at this sentence: “Ten years ago, I remember that my little brother set fire to the house.” The sentence appears to say that your remembering happened ten years ago. Your remembering, in fact, is happening right now: It is your brother’s pyromania that occurred ten years ago. “I remember that ten years ago, my little brother set fire to the house” works well, and is enough warning to your brother’s fiancée.

A temptation in all work is to ignore details. Overlooking the tightening of a lug nut on a car’s tire rim will have obviously bad consequences, and the most elaborately designed turbine engine is only as efficient as the finest fittings of its smallest parts. In writing, however, it is easy to assume that only the Big Ideas matter. But what will take a reader through a big idea are the innumerable details in which it is embedded or expressed. Some of these are matters of easing the way, eliminating awkwardness and thereby giving a reader smooth passage through a skillfully rendered argument. Other touches are enticing on their own: a perfectly chosen adjective, a clean and simple image, a slow and stately sentence, or another that is brief and sharp. Such details begin with the smallest units: words and phrases. But attention to detail dictates as well the larger structures of an essay.

NOT A DRUDGERY

A grammarian once lectured me that no short cut to clear writing exists: It all requires drudgery and workbooks. Thank heaven he was wrong. Here are some shortcuts and other tips that will ease the way.

Before getting to work on an assignment, you might want to take a short break. Do something nice for yourself: Only egotists actually enjoy starting to write. My favorite treat is to eat a lot of Breyer's natural vanilla ice cream while I think a bit about what I have to do. E. B. White, a writer for *The New Yorker* when it was a great and stylish magazine, used to have a martini to loosen up. Not two. *One*. It is a dangerous drink, whether stirred or shaken, and most people might be better off not even knowing of its existence.

A great timesaver might be to start

putting words down soon after you have started to investigate a topic, working on paper or with a computer. Don't be afraid to write down something that you fear may need changing. Remember, you are creating sentences and paragraphs to remold in successive drafts. Once you start writing, keep going. Resist the temptation to get up and check a fact. Leave a blank space to fill in later. The more you get down on paper or a screen, the more likely you are to have usable materials that can later be edited and polished. Whatever you put down may set you to thinking, even if you think only of why what you have just written does not sound right. And the act of putting a bunch of words on paper will reduce your anxiety level about the assignment at hand. Thinking is the ultimate goal, but it is necessary to have something to think about.

The historian Richard Hofstadter, a highly accomplished stylist, once said that the first draft of anything he wrote was a mess. But once he got started, he would tinker with what he had created. He would have profited from a computer. Especially helpful in bringing order out of an untidy start, a computer makes it easy to delete words and substitute new ones, to rearrange sentences in a more logical order, to take your third paragraph and make it your first because it finally occurs to you that this is a better way to begin the paper. Word processing will draw you into editing your own work, and editing or rewriting can actually be a lot of fun, in part because it enhances your self-confidence. Not too many years ago writers had to use scissors and tape to move around parts of their essay.

Let's suppose that in some American Studies course you have been asked to write an essay about Charles Lindbergh, who in May 1927 became the first person to fly solo across the Atlantic Ocean to Europe. Your job is to do some thinking about the meaning of Lindbergh's flight. Relax and see what bobs up to the surface of your mind. Before you get your first real thought on the topic, perhaps you remember that the night before taking off the aviator stopped at a deli to pick up five sandwiches to carry with him in the tiny cockpit of *The Spirit of Saint Louis.* Throwing in even trivia like that will spare you the empty, recriminating stare of a blank page or screen. You then recall that while Lindbergh's plane was over the mid-Atlantic, crystals formed on the wing, indicating that he was in a dangerous ice cloud.

Since writing assignments commonly ask only for significant narrative, you may later delete the first detail, homey though it is. But narrative is often inseparable from analysis, and the story about ice on the plane's wings may suggest a line of thought worth exploring. You need somehow to get acquainted with a man who flew a machine alone 3,342 miles across the Atlantic Ocean amidst storms and fog. Then you can begin to understand that one meaning of the twentieth century reveals itself in Lindbergh's flight. It is the individual and his single-prop engine, the man and the machine, an idea caught in the title of Lindbergh's autobiography: *We.*

SHARE YOUR WORK

I am not suggesting you get your friends to do your work, the way Tom Sawyer cons his into whitewashing the fence for him. Nor do I want to encourage students to believe what my young daughter took from *Mr. Rogers' Neighborhood.* She insisted that she didn't have to learn to swim: Mr. Rogers had announced that she was special. But more profitably for her development, he also told her to share.

After you have done some writing, seek an audience. Anyone will do. Don't worry about criticism. You are learning to write. It's like trying to rollerblade: You are expected to fall many times before becoming good at it. The more suggestions you get that seem sensible to you, the better your essay is likely to be. But the deeper advantage of getting to accept and profit from criticism is self-discovery. You will find out from your readers things that you had not noticed about your own patterns of thought and expression, and hit upon ways of making both more articulate. Telephone your mother: A naturally sympathetic listener can at least assure you that you have said something to someone. More daring is to show your draft to someone you work with or to a roommate; each can be classified as a peer reader. Teachers are authority readers. The reason almost any friend will do to provide initial criticism is that anyone can tell you whether what you have said is clear.

Then you can edit away. Delete some words or phrases, in some cases substitute new ones, move whole sentences around, add material, find more precise wording, explore radically new ways to order your material, have fun. Come back to the passage later, after a short break, or the next day. The novelist Ernest Hemingway offered this advice to writers learning to be self-critical: "The most essential gift for a good writer is a built-in, shockproof shit detector." "What you're doing," wrote the essayist Anne Sexton, "is hunting for what you mean, what you're trying to say." Editing your own work is the way you come to know what it is that you were half-thinking all along.

GAMES IN PLACE OF WORKBOOK EXERCISES

Learning to write well does not have to be dreary, though style manuals try hard to make it so. Such learning is active, not a passive reception of information, and activity, whether physical or intellectual, can be a delight. Most of that enjoyable activity will come after the first difficult minutes of getting started.

At some time in your life you have probably been lectured about needless repetition. You may have heard the words "redundancy" and "tautology." In defining these terms, Webster's *New American College Dictionary*, H. W. Fowler's *Modern English Usage*, and Sheridan Baker's *The Practical Stylist* differ from one another. Unless it is your ambition to become a grammarian, all you really need is an ability to recognize pointless repetition. Can you spot the repetition in each of these phrases?

In my opinion, I think . . .
Necessary essentials
True facts
The rescue team searched for living survivors.
Several people rushed quickly forward.
Dead corpse
Revert back
The secretary very hurriedly scribbled the notes.

If we were to discuss puns to try to instill an interest in language, we could give a Webster's definition: "the humorous use of a word, or of words which are formed or sounded alike but have different meanings, in such a way as to play on two or more of the possible applications." Shakespeare was good at such plays on words, and he didn't even have Webster's to tell him what they were. Here is a pun that illustrates the meaning of that word, and you need to know only that *escargot* is French for “snail”:

> A snail bought a racing car and had a big “S” painted on the side of it. As it sped down the street, people remarked, “Look at the S-car-go.”

For discovering in the English language an endless enjoyment, a curiosity about words is a good starting point. Here are some signs that may take you more than ten seconds to figure out:

A sign on a door:

TOOP
ENDO
ORPU
SH

A sign on a post in New Mexico:

TOTI EMU LESTO

IF YOU CAN THINK, YOU CAN WRITE

That has been an argument of this book. The claim, however, requires an understanding of the single act of thought and writing. A spasm of rage blurted out as "shut up!" is not a thought. It is like blowing a horn in heavy traffic, a primitive noise in the absence of self-control. Neither does good writing have much time for expression of opinion of the sort that starts out "It seems to me that . . ." or "In my opinion . . ." or "I feel that . . ." Now that you are in college few care what you feel. Other students and teachers want to know what you think and why. You have a right to an opinion, even a half-formed one, and to its declaration. What is more important, though, is why you have a particular conviction. If you can argue your way through that, you can think your reasoning onto paper. You can write.

Thought carries itself out in a silent dialogue between you and an imagined companion or antagonist. The dialogue runs through the mind in a kind of invisible script. Transfer that script to paper, delete the useless repetitions, control any wanderings from the main point, get criticisms and edit your work to turn a rough draft into a finished composition, and your thought will be clear, as though you were now having it for the first time.

The best way to understand the principles of composition is to recognize that they are not arbitrary impositions on the process of writing. They are inherent in what thoughts and words do. The act of thinking, speaking, and writing embodies the conventions and the rules. That is why it is good to listen with your mental ear to what is happening in every sentence and every paragraph. You will come to recognize when the words are acting well. Principles and rules are mere descriptions of that well-acting.

Part II

THE STUFF OF WRITING: A GOOD CONVERSATION

Your writing should have the tone of a good conversation. A strategy for achieving this is to attach to concrete incidents and facts an essay's larger theme.

Suppose you have to write something about the exploration of the American West by Meriwether Lewis and William Clark in 1804 under President Thomas Jefferson. It is a subject that should attract students of literature, American civilization, geography, natural science, history, or politics.

Instead of making large generalizations

about Man's Unquenchable Thirst for Discovery, begin, say, with an image of President Jefferson, who commissioned the expedition, as he ponders the mysteries of the Missouri River, the Rocky Mountains, and the Columbia River basin. Rather than announce, "the explorers trudged onward and onward until they reached their destination," fix on describing the party's stubborn progress against the currents of the mighty Missouri River. That, far more than any abstract pronouncements, will establish its dogged heroism. The first leg up the Missouri was an endless poling, pulling, and portaging of a string of boats up a huge river whose powerful current undermined banks at every bend, created mudslides, and sent vast jams of tree trunks cascading downriver to knock over the expedition's boats. Reporting such details is important both for conveying the primitive state of American technology at the time and for revealing the character of the expedition party.

Your beginning paragraph should gently lead the reader into the topic. Any number of approaches will do. That portrayal of Jefferson contemplating the vast stretches of the American West would work. Or you might give a vivid description of men and boats struggling up the Missouri, from which you could backtrack to explain who they were and what they were doing there.

Your opening should in any event be engaging, and it should not sound like a paragraph from a book of instructions on assembling lawn chairs. For this reason, you might avoid the stiff and predictable "The purpose of this paper is. . . ." It is also better to refrain from setting down in your opening paragraph, point by point, the entire argument the rest of the paper will develop. A short indication of your thesis will do. Then let it unfold as the paper develops.

For the paper as a whole, the journey of Lewis and Clark provides ample opportunities for good and interesting writing. Its study of Indian life and culture was a venture into the modern field of ethnology. Members of the party made painstaking studies of the plants and animals of the continental interior, so their trip contributed to the development of natural science. Possessed apparently of no more than a distant acquaintance with Latin, they were beautifully inventive in naming their discoveries, labeling the cutthroat trout, for example, *Salmon clarkii*. That, along with their keeping a journal, makes the expedition an event of landmark significance for American language and literature.

The purpose of the final paragraph in an essay is to bring it to a graceful finish. It therefore should not involve any lengthy restating of your argument, as though your readers have too short an attention span to remember what you have just finished telling them. You need not, for instance, announce that the exploration was courageous, inventive, and alive with scientific curiosity. A reader who hasn't figured that out by now cannot be rescued. But suppose you want to pay some final tribute to this remarkable adventure. How about a brief reference to the first moon landing? The two expeditions have enough in common, and yet sufficiently differ, that some deft comparisons should allow you to ponder for a final moment the character and accomplishments of Jefferson's explorers.

Compare the two indented introductions presented here. The first is the work of a student who wishes simply to begin a freshman paper and falls back on a standard format that succeeds in being both lecturish and boring. The second suggests that the expedition lives in the imagination of a writer who wants it to come to life for the reader as well. Though longer, it is more economical of words, for the writer manages to convey concretely not only the topic but some of the factual background that would otherwise have to come up later in the paper. The route from the mechanical first introduction to the more inviting second opening cannot be traveled overnight. But like the expedition of Lewis and Clark, it is worth making.

I

Exploration is a frequent event in history. One of the most important expeditions in the American past was the journey of Meriwether Lewis and William Clark into the North American West. The purpose of this paper is to describe the exploration. It will tell about its anthropological, biological, and literary achievements. Then the paper will compare Lewis and Clark with more recent explorers.

II

In 1803 President Thomas Jefferson bought from France one of the world's most splendid scientific laboratories. The vast Louisiana Purchase, defined by the Mississippi River to the east and by a jagged line running northwestward from New Orleans, promised to most interested Americans lands to settle or natural riches to exploit.

But it also abounded in plants and animals unknown to European scholars, along with Indian tribes whose ways and customs invited investigation. Perhaps, thought Jefferson, the great mammoths were not extinct but grazed on western grasses. Possibly too the llama, native to South America, had found a home in those northern stretches. And what lay to the west of Louisiana, in territories under the claim of Spain, Britain, and Russia?

The relentlessly curious Jefferson determined to find out. Meriwether Lewis and William Clark, military rather than scientific men, received his commission to explore the North American West. So began one of the most remarkable adventures in the nation's history.

Now here are two paragraphs that could end the paper. Again, the second stretches the scope of the reader's imagination in a way that the first cannot do.

I

Lewis and Clark were great explorers. They made great contributions to anthropology, natural science, and geography. Their

journey was heroic. Many American enterprises since, such as the moon landing in 1969 of Neil Armstrong and Edwin Aldrin with the assistance of Mike Collins, have continued their legacy of heroism and adventure.

II

On July 20, 1969, Neil Armstrong and Edwin "Buzz" Aldrin walked on the moon's surface, while their colleague Mike Collins assisted from the spacecraft that had carried them. They stood not amidst rich vegetation but on an airless desert, and they gathered cold rocks for scientists to analyze. While Lewis and Clark had wandered far from the settled regions of the republic, the moon pioneers were in constant radio communication with earth control. The skills they wielded were not the inventive survival techniques of Jefferson's explorers but the sophisticated devices of twentieth-century science and technology. Yet in their combination of scientific curiosity and private daring, they represented the transplantation into our own times of the mind and character of their Jeffersonian forebears.

WORDS

In this next paragraph cross out unnecessary words, substituting shorter phrases if necessary and combining sentences when you can. After you have given your best effort, and only then, reward yourself by turning to the next page for a suggested revision.

That winter there was a great amount of snow. The weight of it made the branches of trees sag. Great drifts piled around and on top of cars and made them impossible to move. Ice formed on windows, which became stuck, and no one would be able to open them until late February. Pedestrians lost their footing on sidewalks that had layers and layers of ice on them, and disgruntled householders had to clear away their driveways, even though within just twenty-four hours a new snow was sure to fall and cover the drive ways all over again and they would have to be shoveled anew.

Here's a trimmed-down version of the paragraph on the preceding page.

That winter snow after snow weighed down the branches of trees, while cars lay imprisoned beneath cold white drifts. Windows were stuck from the ice that had formed upon them; not until late February would they become free. The ice on sidewalks sent pedestrians skidding, and disgruntled householders cleared snow from their driveways, even though within the next twenty-four hours new snow would cover them again.

Is that the very best the writer can do? Try to make the paragraph even more concise.

That winter snow after snow weighed down the branches of trees and imprisoned cars beneath cold white drifts. Ice locked windows in a grip that would not relax until late February. Pedestrians skidded on glassy sidewalks, and householders muttered as they cleared their driveways of snow that within twenty-four hours a new storm would replace.

Spotting unnecessary words, such as "great amount" and "around and on top" in the first version of the paragraph, was a small if essential part of the effort. The more important job was to find direct substitutes for loose phrases. "Windows were stuck from the ice" in the second version is a slow beginning to a sentence that in the final revision starts with the crisp "Ice locked windows."

Look for the smallest opportunity to trim prose. An obvious place to spot unnecessary terms is within strings of descriptive words. Even words that differ in tone or meaning may not differ sufficiently to justify their pairing. "From birth, he was assured a splendid and magnificent future." "Splendid" and "magnificent" are not quite identical in meaning, but are they really so far apart that the writer has to use both? You may need a sharper lens to recognize that in "Besides forgetting my phone number, I also lost my address book," "Besides" by itself does all the work that "also" is meant to do.

"Simplify, simplify, simplify," Henry David Thoreau wrote in *Walden*. Simplicity goes with the trimming of words, and elegance is their joint achievement. Never pass up a chance to press a loose expression into a more compact phrase. "Because of my excitement, I kept awake" should give way to "Excitement kept me awake." For "Worries that had been with me for a long time made me stay awake," substitute, "My old worries kept me awake." Be direct and positive: "He was not very often on time" becomes "He was usually late."

The greatest respect a writer can show to words, then, is to be sparing in their use and attentive in their choice. From time to time, of course, careful selection may dictate a longer rather than a shorter expression. "The wind made me drop my books" is less effective than "The wind whipped the books from my hands."

Here are a few suggestions about the choice of specific words:

■ Search for words or phrases that will give energy to your writing. Get a feeling, above all, for the force and texture of words. For "I became excited and that influenced my speech," substitute "Emotions jumbled my words." Develop a liking for words that evoke the senses: taste, touch, hearing, sight, smell. In place of "all the sounds in the forest made him nervous," say, "at every snap of a twig, every flutter of a wing, his nerves jumped." Concrete words evoking tangible or visible things or actions rather than ideas strengthen writing. "He wept" is better than "He was sorrowful." But in avoiding flat expressions, don't fill your essays with flashy phrases that merely draw attention to your belief in your own brilliance. "The scorching sun of the long afternoon drew sweat from my body" can give way to "Through the long afternoon, I sweated."

■ Avoid clichés, those phrases worked to death that people fall back on when imagination fails them: "water over the dam," "generous to a fault," "dead as a doornail," "cool as a cucumber," "selling like hotcakes," "like a bat out of hell," "in-depth analysis," "key players," "window of opportunity," "meaningful," "feedback," "cutting edge."

■ What does "in terms of" mean? It fails to

make clear what relationship it is trying to designate. Suppose someone announces, "I want to talk about this country's foreign relations in terms of the future." Are you going to hear about how the nation's foreign relations will affect its future, or what its future foreign relations should be, or what they will be?

■ Talk to your reader. How many people do you know who in a spoken conversation would use "i.e.," meaning "that is"? And the piling of nouns one upon another, such as "sense response activation," suggests an effort to appear professional or intellectually deep. Instead of saying the roundabout "The following passage illustrates . . . ," try "Here is a passage that illustrates my point." Then quote it.

■ The words "fortunately" and "unfortunately" are seldom if ever useful. They give a reader unnecessary instructions on how to think. Why would anyone need to say, "Fortunately, I got over my illness," or "Unfortunately, the epidemic killed many people"? What hope is left for anyone who has to be told that a fatal epidemic is unfortunate?

■ Avoid distracting parentheses as much as you can, and especially avoid this kind: "He (Smith) agreed." If any doubt exists about whom "he" refers to, just write, "Smith agreed," even if this constitutes a repetition of "Smith."

■ The word "hopefully," as in "Hopefully, you'll get well," should give way to the bold "I hope you get well" or "I hope it will be sunny today." "Hopefully, I'll catch the bus" could mean either that it is to be hoped you'll catch it or that when you catch it you'll be in a hopeful mood.

GRACE AND FLOW

Good writing flows. It may have the smooth fluency of a mountain brook in the spring runoff. Or it may be a river's angry rush over a streambed of rocks. Here are some ways, beyond the choice of words, that you can promote its flowing. For each principle, see whether your ear for good speech approves.

■ Finding just the right opening for an essay is difficult and requires special attention. As you read or listen to a lecture, be on guard for ideas or facts that would make a good beginning.

■ A paragraph should develop or illustrate an idea. Although on occasion even a paragraph of one sentence will be appropriate, too many brief paragraphs of the kind often found in newspapers give writing a jerky effect.

■ Subheadings do not help much to organize your essay. They are artificial devices for supplying an order that your writing itself should have attended to. A mild substitute for subheadings is to leave a space between sections of your paper that involve a great separation in theme. This manual does use subheadings, but that is because its purpose does not allow it to be a unified essay.

■ Try not to bore the reader with the wooden "First" ("Firstly" sounds even worse), "Second," "Third," "Fourth," and so on. Simple English prose will do the same job as tired numbering systems that merely show you can count the fingers of at least one hand. Expressions such as *also, moreover, for example, yet,* and *however* can move your prose from point to point, but don't clutter your essay with these words. The logic and sequence of your argument itself should govern the prose.

■ Be attentive to how phrases in a sentence can best fit together. Consider the sentence "He gained the respect and friendship of many skeptical people by his generosity." The phrase "by his generosity" is too distantly separated from the verb "gained." Try instead, "His generosity won him the respect and friendship of many skeptical people." What phrase is out of place in this sentence: "She raised the emotions of those who listened to her impassioned talk to a new pitch"? The answer is "to a new pitch," which should follow "raised."

■ Combine short, choppy sentences: "He believed that the plan would be unpopular. He therefore argued for a delay." Try this: "Believing that the plan would be unpopular, he argued for a delay."

■ At the same time, disassemble whatever long sentences are loose and wandering: "Looking to his political future, he entered into an alliance with his earlier opponents, who soon broke with him because while he was useful as a speaker he was indiscreet in his private life." Here's a fix: "Looking to his political future, he entered into an alliance with his earlier opponents. But while they found him useful as a speaker, they soon broke with him over his private indiscretions."

■ Length in a sentence, however, is not in itself a vice. A very long sentence with phrases in perfect balance may carry the reader along as smoothly as shorter ones and gain majesty from its very length. The opening sentence of the Declaration of Independence, with its grand beginning "When, in the course of human events, . . ." occupies a whole paragraph. The second sentence, starting with "We hold these truths to be self-evident" and proceeding to define those self-evident truths, is even longer. Yet the two sentences are models of clarity and persuasiveness. A sentence may be as long as you please, provided you confine it to a single series of connected ideas and by careful punctuation and balance avoid tedious confusion.

■ As a general rule—but only after checking a sentence carefully for sound and meaning—put its main section toward the end. "I was exhausted after ten hours of heavy labor in the field" ends less sharply and firmly than "After ten hours of heavy labor in the field, I was exhausted." An even better correction is "Ten hours of heavy labor in the field left me exhausted."

■ Resist mixing or scrambling images. "The idea sprouted in my mind like a flower and ran away with me" forces the reader to imagine a running flower. Do not confuse that error with a legitimate construction that sounds a great deal like it. "He soared above his enemies; in combat he was a lion; among even his most hardened opponents he was a shark among toothless prey." Lions, of course, do not soar, and neither birds nor lions swim like fish. But the sentence is acceptable, for each of the three images is clearly separate from the others.

■ Catching repetition in phrases such as "necessary essentials" is pretty easy. But it can also occur, more seriously, in circular statements such as "She was known for her industriousness because she had gained a reputation for working hard." Here the second part of the sentence essentially repeats the first, so that nothing is learned, no information imparted.

■ Before repeating a word frequently in the same paragraph, make sure that you have justification for doing so. Repetition leads a reader to conclude that you have not thought out what you wanted to say, but rather have let the word echo meaninglessly from sentence to sentence. Variation is a sign to your readers that you are alert. Absentmindedly repeating the same construction at the beginning of consecutive or neighboring sentences can have a similarly ill effect. "Wishing to finish my work, I stayed up late. Hoping to spot all my mistakes, I read and reread my essay." To correct the repetition, you might change "Hoping to spot" to "In hopes of spotting."

■ "It is interesting to note that. . . ." What a wordy, windy phrase! Just proceed directly to noting what you wish to note. The belief in a style appropriate to academic discourse is probably a major cause of violations of good writing. And leave confusing statements to politicians. President Richard Nixon once said to the press: "I know you believe you understand what you think I said, but I am not sure you realize that what you heard is not what I meant." Strive for the directness that Sherlock Holmes achieves: "I never guess, Watson."

■ Your ear will hear that the active sentence "Jackie Robinson caught the ball" has more energy than the passive sentence "The ball was caught by Jackie Robinson." And "The committee reached a decision" beats out "A decision was reached by the committee."

■ "Her first article and her most important book were published in 1976 and 1982 respectively." Here "respectively" is the writer's lazy instruction to the reader to go back over the sentence and fix the right year to the right publication. Write simply, "Her first article was published in 1976, and her most important book in 1982."

■ A good reader or writer will catch grating sounds. You may, for example, have accidentally written, "The administr*ation* is setting up st*ations* for registr*ation*." Is the sentence structurally flawed? Not at all. Is the sentence unclear? If the material preceding it lets the reader know what is being discussed, it is perfectly clear. Here the repetition of the "*ation*" is simply annoying. Words that rhyme or jingle should not creep close together. For a revision, you could write, "The administration is setting up registration posts."

■ Proofread your work. Serious writers proofread until the final second, and a good instructor will allow you neatly to ink in corrections on a final draft. Every writer makes some typographical errors. A writer too lazy or sloppy to correct these mistakes may offend readers, who sometimes make quick, lasting judgments in reaction to mistakes careless writers regard as inconsequential. Rather than read it on the screen or trust a computer's spellcheck to catch everything, you may find it convenient to print a hard copy of an essay for proofreading.

SOME LIMITS EVEN LIBERATED WRITERS HAVE TO ACCEPT

This manual has avoided technical grammatical terms, such as *intransitive verb, demonstrative pronoun, predicate adjective, correlative conjunction, conjunctive adverb, subordinating conjunction, comma splice,* and *dependent clauses with relative pronouns.* But here are some principles, fundamental to the structure of the English language, that a writer must become acquainted with. Once more, we encourage you to sense their reasonableness, to test each by your inherent knowledge of English.

■ A logical sense can spot what grammarians call dangling or misplaced modifiers. They are among the most common errors. Here's an example: "A clumsy fool, people nonetheless tolerate me." This sentence unintentionally says that people are a clumsy fool. The writer might better say, "A clumsy fool, I nonetheless am tolerated." What is wrong with this next sentence: "Upon entering the doctor's office, a skeleton caught my attention"? Remember that the knowledge of what's wrong with it is already within you. If you can see that the sentence has a skeleton enter a doctor's office, you don't need to keep in mind the phrase "dangling modifier." "Happy to be going to Boston, his bus ride was pleasant" says that the bus ride was happy to be going to Boston. Try, "Happy to be going to Boston, he had a pleasant bus ride." Anything wrong with "After working all day, the desk got finished" or "Inspecting the books, the error was immediately apparent"?

■ The problem can be a little harder to catch. Recognize the logical flaw in this quite common use of "based": "Based on the forecaster's careful calculations, next year's rainfall will be heavy." That says that the rain itself is based on the forecaster's careful calculations. A similar mistake that you will encounter is in the use of "due to." "Due to the rain, little Murgatroyd stayed home" says that little Murgatroyd was due to the rain.

■ An attentive ear will give you a feeling for keeping essentially alike the elements in a series. "The construction crew worked hard, surrendered free time, and it succeeded in completing the job on time." Just get rid of the "it" before "succeeded" and the items in the series will be parallel: "worked . . . surrendered . . . succeeded."

■ Note the problem of balance in this sentence: "He is neither foolhardy nor is he a coward." Can you see why, even apart from its greater economy of words, this sentence is better: "He is neither foolhardy nor a coward"? The same trouble can occur with "either . . . or," "both . . . and," "between . . . and," and "not only . . . but." Look for the flaw in each of these sentences: "She was both tired and she was cranky"; "I will be either better today or tomorrow"; "He not only stole from the company but he framed another employee." Remember that the knowledge of what is wrong in these sentences lies within you, in the sense of English that speaking, hearing, and reading has implanted in you. Bring that sense to the surface.

■ The words "like," "unlike," "similar," "in contrast," "in addition," and "besides" should connect the things you want to connect. "In contrast to last year, my work is going well" announces that my work is in contrast to a year.

■ Reason, reinforced by a good ear, will warn you that something is wrong with the sentence "He did not finish yet." You want "He has not finished yet," which accurately and pleasingly brings the non-finishing right up to the present and keeps it from ending or drifting away some time in the past. The simple verb "lost" in "She discovered she lost her wallet" must give way to "had lost," which correctly puts the losing at an earlier time than the discovering. If somewhere in an essay you have to drop into a past time earlier than the time you have been talking about, set yourself into the earlier time with a "have" or "had" verb: "has not finished," "had lost." Then you will be free to go to simple past tense verbs for the remainder of your narrative of that earlier past.

■ Make sure pronouns agree with the nouns they refer to. If you say, "The psychology conference convened late in 1991," you can't go on to remark, "Their objective was to figure out why children like peanut butter and jelly." The word "conference" takes the singular "its," not the plural "their." If you write, "The kindergarten class is playing on the lawn," you cannot for the next sentence forget that "class" requires not "they" or "their" but "it" or "its."

PRONOUNS: THE MISSING YEARS OF MIDDLE SCHOOL

Using correct personal pronouns can be tedious. But when someone who is interviewing you for a job knows how to use them, you may wish you did.

Students used to learn a foreign language not by speaking it as many do today, but by mastering its grammar. That way they learned, if they had not already learned from English grammar, the difference between the "subjective" (or "nominative") and the "objective" case. The subject names an actor; the object, the person or thing receiving the action. In "I hit him," "I" is the subject, "him" the object.

This chart shows the subjective and objective forms of pronouns ("it" and "you" do not change forms):

Subjective	Objective
I	me
he	him
she	her
who	whom
we	us
they	them

The objective case of a pronoun is appropriate in only three situations:

■ The objective case applies to a pronoun that is the object of a preposition, as in "Do this for me" (you would have to have a dented tin ear to say or write, "Do this for

I"). Here is a list of common prepositions: *about, above, across, after, against, along, among, around, as, at, before, behind, below, beneath, besides, between, beyond, concerning, despite, down, during, except, for, from, in, into, like, near, next to, of, off, on, opposite, over, through, to, toward, under, up, upon, with.*

■ When the pronoun is the object of an infinitive, the objective case is needed. An infinitive is merely the word "to" followed by a verb. You say, "I would like to find her," not "I would like to find she."

■ The objective case governs a pronoun that is the object, either direct or indirect, of a verb: when the person or thing the pronoun refers to receives directly or indirectly the action represented by the verb.

Direct object: "Ethel brought him home."

Indirect object: "David Runk gave me a surprise party." ("Party" is the direct object here.)

In writing and even in speaking, a good user of the language will be careful to maintain the distinctions between subjective and objective pronouns. "Him and me work hard" incorrectly employs the objective in place of "He and I." Perhaps in a misguided attempt to be formal, on the other hand, people frequently but quite incorrectly say, "between he and I"; the correct usage is "between him and me."

In all forms of the verb "to be" except the infinitive, the formal rule is that the pronoun following the verb is to be in the nominative: "The people most responsible are we." Usage permits an exception. In informal conversation, the objective forms "it's me," "it's her," and so forth have the easier and more pleasant sound.

Part III

A BRIEF GLOSSARY

A formal adherence to rules will not by itself make you a good writer, nor will violations necessarily make you a bad one. Superior writing can blithely and even beautifully go contrary to all sorts of rules. Great poetry in particular often flagrantly disobeys grammar rules. The best service rules can perform, perhaps, is to make you think closely about words and their interplay. Rules, then, should get you to a point at which you can be free of rules. "Grammar," wrote the essayist Joan Didion, "is a piano I play by ear." Every effort is made here to express simply and plainly some points of style and grammar that you should hold in mind.

above and **below, former** and **latter**—Effective writing does not refer back or forward.

Instead of speaking of "the above graph" or "the graph below," number graphs and tables 1.1, 1.2, and so on, and then refer to Table 1.1 or Table 1.2. Avoid also such uses of "former" and "latter" as "The latter passage needs clarification." Instead, say "That passage about [whatever]. . . ." It is, of course, legitimate to refer to someone as the "former editor of the paper."

accept, except—"Accept" means "receive"; "except" as a verb means "exclude."

adjectives and **adverbs**—Whenever you use two or more adverbs or adjectives instead of one, make sure that each has a separate and needed meaning. Often, as in "perky, animated Drusilla," one or the other can be eliminated.

affect, effect—"Affect" as a verb means "influence": "The news did not much affect me." "Effect" as a verb means "cause," "bring about": "The news effected no change in my plans." As a noun, "effect" refers to an influence: "The news had little effect on me." "Affect" as a noun is in use by psychologists for referring to a person's ability to articulate emotions.

all together and **altogether**—"All together" means "in a group," as in "At last the old friends, so long separated, were all together." "Altogether" means "entirely": "I skipped lunch altogether."

alot—For "alot," which is not a word, substitute "a lot."

ambiguity (lack of a clear meaning or reference): "I reached for the horse's bridle, but it ran away." Readers will know, of course, that the horse and not the bridle ran away. But the split second during which their mental ear attaches "it" to the bridle and then has to shift to the horse will be an annoyance. "It" and other pronouns can be unclear in reference: "Tom and the horse were waiting for the day's trail ride, but he looked unfriendly." Here are some more illustrations of ambiguity, in this case presumably intentional, from a professor who might make such remarks in what pass as letters of recommendation: "I most enthusiastically recommend this candidate with no qualifications whatsoever"; "In my opinion you will be very fortunate to get this person to work for you"; "I would urge you to waste no time in making this applicant an offer of employment."

and/or—Sheridan Baker in *The Practical Stylist* calls this graceless thing an "ungainly thought stopper." Except occasionally in legal or technical writing, "or" will do.

apposition—A word or phrase is in apposition to another when it immediately follows to explain or identify. "Bill Clinton, the world's greatest saxophonist, looked like a balloon."

area—Stick to using this word for physical spaces. "In the area of scholarship" means "in scholarship"; "thorough in all areas" means "thorough." Similarly, "large in size" means "large."

as—Say, "Nobody despises you as I do," not "Nobody despises you like I do." But avoid "as" when you mean "since" or "because." "As it was late, I went home" is a weak substitute for "Since it was late, . . ."

aspect—As in the poet William Wordsworth's use of "aspect" in *Tintern Abbey*, the word means literally "view." "Facet" refers to a face of a diamond. When used in substitution for "part" or "component," these words threaten to become jargon. See **jargon.**

at—The "at" in "where at" or "Where is he at?" is unneeded. The "where" includes the meaning of "at." The word "whence" contains a built-in "from": "Whence"—not "From whence"—"have they come?"

authored—Write instead, "she wrote a play."

be sure and, try and—Use "be sure to" and "try to."

between, among—A simple rule is to employ "between" with two items and "among" with more than two: "between the two of us"; "among the three of us."

bibliographies—Alphabetize them by authors' last names.

both—In the sentence "He was both happy as well as puzzled," "both" and "as well as" mean the same thing. Delete either "both" or "as well as" (substituting "and" for "as well as").

can, may—"Can" refers to ability and "may" seeks permission. "Can you swim?" "May I help you?"

capital, capitol—The capitol—note the "o"—is the domed building in Washington, D.C., or the statehouse buildings in Albany, Sacramento, Austin, and elsewhere. "Capital" is used for everything else.

cite, site—To cite is to quote an authority; a site is a particular location.

colon (:)—Use it before a list of things or to expand on the earlier part of a sentence.

commas (,) denote logical separation or pauses. "Roland, you need a breath mint." Most writers use the comma to separate all the items in a series: "I like bread, butter, and strawberry jam." Commas should set off information not essential to the meaning of the sentence: "The best way to see Cadillac Mountain, unless you are pressed for time, is to climb it." Commas also go before parts of long sentences that are connected by "and," "but," or "or." The commas go before these words, not after them: "She was awkward in an attractive sort of way, and he was not without redeeming merit, all things considered."

compared to, compared with—When you liken one thing to another, employ "compare to": "In size, New York compares more closely to Tokyo than to Munich." In examining two things to determine their differences as well as their similarities, make it "compared with": "Compared with the troubles other people face, mine begin to look insignificant."

complement, compliment—"Complement" means "go well with" or "complete"; a compliment is a flattering remark, and a complimentary book is free of charge.

consensus of opinion means consensus.

contact—Don't contact people. Phone them, write them, see them, find them, look them up, tell them, meet them.

contractions—Words like "doesn't" or "can't" are fine in speech or even the informal prose in which this book is written, but in formal prose avoid them as you would slang.

"could of" in place of "could have" persists among some college students. Also watch out for "should of," "would of," "may of," "must of," and "might of." Each gets "have," not "of."

credible, credulous, creditable—"Credible" means "believable": "The news that he has once more stolen from his partners is completely credible." "Credulous" means "naive, quick to believe": "In thinking that this time he could be trusted, his partners were astonishingly credulous." "Creditable" refers to an action that reflects well on the actor: "Giving back the money is the most creditable thing he has ever done."

criteria, curricula, data—All of these are plural. "Criterion," "curriculum," and "datum" are the singular forms.

dash (—)—Use dashes to set off an interruption in a long sentence, usually a digression or piece of extra information. Dashes may interrupt the flow of writing less than putting material in parentheses. But don't use dashes frequently.

diction—This word refers to choice of words and grammatical constructions, not to pronunciation.

discreet, discrete—A discreet person is careful and sensitive: "He is always discreet, and I know that he will keep their secret." A thing that is clearly separate is discrete: "He made not a single argument but three discrete claims."

disinterested, uninterested—"Disinterested" means not "uninterested" but "able to act justly, without considerations of self-interest." A disinterested judge will be attentive, caring, wise, and fair; an uninterested judge would be cold and detached from the proceedings.

double space—Type papers in double spaces and leave plenty of margin for the instructor's comments.

each, either, everybody, everyone, no one, none (when meaning not one), **somebody, someone** take singular verbs. For the gender implications of this rule, see the entry **his/her.** If the word "or" separates two parts of a sentence, the verb agrees with the noun closer to it.

each other—Use the phrase in reference to two; use "one another" for three or more.

east—When indicating regions, capitalize **North, South, East, West, Northeast, Southeast, Northwest, Southwest**, but in referring to direction ("they traveled three hundred miles east"), use the lower case. Whether to capitalize "eastern, northern, western, southern," and the like is up to you, though the modern tendency is not to capitalize these words.

ellipsis (. . .)—An elipsis is the omission of a word, or several words, in a quoted passage. The use of three periods, or points of ellipsis, within a quotation signifies that something nonessential is being omitted. (Include spaces before and after each period unless the first one is at the end of a sentence, and in that case the first period is added to the other three.)

emigrate, immigrate—You emigrate from a country; you immigrate to your new homeland.

end product, end result—Skip the word "end."

enthuse is a cooey, gushy nonword.

equally as good—Say instead, "equally good" or "as good as."

euphemisms are relatively pleasant words substituted for harsher ones: "correctional facility" for "prison." Their use often betrays a desire to appear refined.

exclamation points used excessively are tiresome, and double and triple exclamation points are amateurish.

facility—Just say what the thing is: "He is a guard at the prison," not "the prison facility."

the fact that—Avoid the phrase unless you are being paid by the word.

farther, further—Restrict "farther" to references to physical distance and save "further" for quantity or degree. "Ethel walked farther into the woods than the girl named Will-o-the-wisp"; "Most parents require further instruction in operating the VCR."

fewer, less—"Fewer" is used for numbers of things, and "less" in relation to a single substance or thing: "fewer soup bowls," "less soup."

finalize—Avoid this ugly, pretentious word, along with "prioritize."

fortuitous means "happening by chance" as well as "happening by good fortune."

founder, flounder—A sinking ship founders and is gone; a fish called a flounder flops about, and so a person who acts or speaks uncertainly, or in a confused and vacillating manner, is said to flounder.

fulsome means not "full" but "disgusting."

hanged, hung—People are hanged; pictures are hung on a wall.

his/her, she/he, s/he and other phrases for acknowledging the equality of the female gender make for clumsy usage that interrupts thought. Even "he or she," now in common use, is not a graceful solution, especially when it has to be repeated. Some writers, in referring to no particular person, go back and forth between "he," and "she," but a reader may find this to be too self-conscious a statement of gender equality. When "she" is used instead of "he" to indicate equality, "she" is surprising even to the modern ear and therefore graceless. To avoid such devices and yet keep clear of language you think to be sexist and therefore offensive, you can always find a way to rewrite the sentence. One easy device usually available is to put everything in the plural.

The sentence "Everyone always tries to get their way" presents a similar problem. The word "everyone" and other singulars mentioned under "each" in this alphabetical list still demand a singular pronoun. A writer who realizes that "his" as referring to both sexes is now jarring but recognizes the awkwardness of "his or her" may choose completely to rework the sentence. In place of "Everyone always demands to get his or her way," you might write, "No one is considerate enough of the needs of others." Conservatives may argue that the antisexist impulse tends to deny the existence of two sexes in the human species. But the English language is palpably sexist, and some traditional linguistic practices are simply bigoted. Adding the suffix "ess" to poet, author, or Jew is offensive. The words "empress" and "goddess," however, are unlikely to carry a disparaging effect.

however, moreover, therefore—For smoother writing, put these words neither at the beginning nor at the end of sentences. In the case of "however," you might begin a sentence instead with a simple "But." An exception: "However" in the sense of "in whatever way" can come at the beginning: "However she tried, she could not learn German."

ibid., a term meaning "same as before," appears in footnotes, but is now falling into disuse. Many scholars prefer to repeat a shortened version of the original title. Today "ibid." is rarely italicized.

infer, imply—The writer implies, or suggests, while the reader infers, or draws a conclusion.

inflated phrases—Avoid "at the present time" for "now," "by means of" for "by," "due to the fact that" for "since" (or "because"), "for the purpose of" for "for," "for the reason that" for "since" (or "because"), "in order to" for "to," "in the event that" for "if," and "until such time as" for "until."

ingenious, ingenuous—A highly inventive person is ingenious; a person innocently direct and honest is ingenuous.

irregardless is not a word.

italicizing—The English language is rich enough that you can usually avoid italicizing words for emphasis. Sometimes an author italicizes part of a quotation to draw particular attention to it; in such a case be sure to say [italics added] after you add them. Italicize titles of books, magazines, newspapers, plays, films, paintings, and other works of art, as well as names of trains, airplanes, and ships, including starships like the *Enterprise*.

its is the possessive or ownership form of "it": "The car had a tear in one of its tires." "It's" is a contraction bringing together "it" and "is": "It's going to be a warm summer." Note also the differences among these words: "their," "there," and they're"; "to," "too," and "two." In letters applying for jobs or essays submitted to graduate schools, mistakes like these can be fatal.

jargon—The specialized terminology of bureaucrats or people in a particular discipline, which is often incomprehensible to the uninitiated. It is puffed-up language. Examples include "viable" for "workable" and "facilitate" for "help." To vary your vocabulary, you can occasionally use such words, but relying on them will give your essay a stuffy tone.

lay, lie, lying—Dogs lie down by the fire. Yesterday they lay down by the fire. Magazines are found lying on the table. People lay money on the table; a week ago they laid money on the table.

margins on an essay—Keep the left- and right-hand margins roughly the same width, usually from an inch to an inch and a half.

non sequitur (Latin for "it does not follow") refers to a statement that is presented as if it follows logically from one just preceding, while it does not in fact do so: "He is supremely confident of his abilities, and he should get the job of nuclear waste inspector."

notetaking for a research paper—For the sake of your sanity, use only one side of a piece of paper. You may want to put your notes on 5″ × 8″ cards, since they are large enough that you can write on them fairly extensively and small enough that rubber bands go around them easily. Begin each card or set of cards with a full bibliographical citation: author, title, place of publication, publisher, and date of publication. Always be sure that your name and phone number are on the top of your packet as well as on the inside cover of your textbooks. For safety make a photocopy of your notes after each day's work or transfer them to a computer hard drive and a floppy disk.

number pages in your essay.

numbers—Write out numbers at the beginning of a sentence and those under 101; that's the rule in *The Chicago Manual of Style*, a standard reference book. Exception: when a whole lot of numbers appear in a paragraph, they can be put in Arabic (32, 2, 961).

only—The placement of "only" within a sentence can alter the meaning. The oldtime popular song "I Only Have Eyes for You" should have been "I Have Eyes for You Only."

possessive—When one noun names a person or thing belonging to another person or thing, an apostrophe (') shows the ownership: "baby's teether," "Jones's house." When the noun denoting the owner is of two or more syllables and ends in "s," the apostrophe alone will do without an extra "s": "Hutchins'." To make the possessive of plural nouns, simply add "s'"; or in the case of a noun ending in "s," simply the apostrophe. For an exception, see **its.**

principal, principle—A principal runs the high school; a principle is a theory or governing idea.

quotation marks (" ")—Use them sparingly; try to save them for real quotations. A period or comma goes inside quotation marks, a semicolon or colon outside. A question mark goes outside unless it's part of the material being quoted.

quotations—Indent and single-space quotations of four or more lines and use a full line space before and after. When quotations are indented, omit quotation marks unless they appear within the material you are quoting. Keep quotations short, merge them smoothly into the text where possible, and in the body of your essay identify their source. Some readers skip lengthy quotations, and an instructor is primarily interested in your own ideas. Anything quoted must be faithfully reproduced with deadly accuracy. If the text you are reproducing quotes someone else, use single quotation marks surrounding that passage unless the larger passage is indented. In spoken or informal language, "quote" is in common use as a noun, but "quotation" is preferable in formal prose.

remains to be seen—Everything from this second on remains to be seen, so the phrase adds nothing to an essay.

research papers—A tip: Concentrate in general on more recent scholarly books and articles; these tend to recapitulate older studies, and so to a certain extent—though by no means entirely—may make it unnecessary to consult all the older work.

ribbons or cartridges—Typewriter and computer ribbons or cartridges wear out and eventually have to be replaced. It is difficult to read a paper printed with a worn-out cartridge.

a semicolon (;) separates longer independent clauses that are not connected by "and," "or," or "but." An independent clause has a subject, a verb, and a complete thought, and so could stand alone as a sentence. A semicolon can also separate groups of words within each of which commas already divide the words.

simplistic means "oversimplified," not merely "simple."

split infinitives—These occur when any word comes between "to" and a verb: they are common and may be usable when the writer wishes to emphasize the inserted word, but tend toward triteness: "to really know," "to better understand."

stationary, stationery—If you are stationary, you are standing still. You write on stationery such as paper.

syntax is the arrangement and interrelationship of words in a sentence.

than, then—"Than" is used in comparisons: "New York is larger than San Francisco." "Then" denotes time: "I was then ready to go to the nightclub."

there is and **there are** have legitimate uses but may delay your getting to your subject.

transpire means "be emitted" as a vapor, hence "leak out" or "become known," and should not be used as a fancy synonym for "happen."

uniqueness admits of no degrees. You cannot be somewhat pregnant. You cannot be a little bit dead. In the same way something can't be nearly unique.

very—Use infrequently.

which, that—"That" introduces a restrictive clause, a limiting or defining set of words: "The house that caught fire belonged to the mayor." The phrase "that caught fire" tells which house is under discussion. Note that the phrase requires no commas. "Which" introduces a nonrestrictive clause adding information not essential to the main part of the sentence: "My house on the corner, which is sixty years old, caught fire."

who, that—Say "the woman who blew away," but "the house that blew away."

COMMON SCHOLARLY ABBREVIATIONS

A.D.—Anno Domini, "in the year of our Lord" (use *preceding* date)

anon.—anonymous

B.C.—before Christ (*following* date)

B.C.E.—before the common, current, or Christian era: the equivalent of B.C.

c., ca.—about (usually referring to time)

C.E.—common, current, or Christian era: the equivalent of A.D.

cap or cap.—capitalize

cf.—compare

e.g.—for example

ed.—editor, edited, edition

et al.—and others

etc.—and so forth (the "et" in "etcetera" is Latin—and French—for "and")

f.—the page that follows

ff.—the pages that follow

fl.—flourished: refers to the time in which an individual, a people, a culture, or a nation was at greatest vigor, creativity, or self-assertion.

i.e.—that is

infra—below

l.c.—put a letter in lowercase (uncap); u.c., uppercase

MS—manuscript

MSS—manuscripts

N.B.—*nota bene*, please note

n.d.—no date

n.pl.—no place of publication

p.—page

passim—here and there

pp.—pages

rev.—revised

sic—thus: to show that the passage you are quoting has an error in the original: "Many people has [*sic*] trouble with grammar."

stet—Latin for "let it stand"; like *ibid., stet* is so common in English that it often stands without italics.

viz—namely

vol.—volume

PROOFREADING SIGNS

Some proofreading signs that editors often use are:

= close up space

= insert comma

= insert letter, word, or sentence

= insert period

= insert space

= paragraph

= insert semicolon

= insert apostrophe

= insert open quotes

= insert closed quotes

= insert hyphen

= insert dash (show length)

= delete and close up

stet = let it stand

tr = transpose

cap = capitalize

Part IV

SUCCEEDING IN COLLEGE COURSES

STUDYING A SUBJECT AND STUDYING FOR EXAMS

The instructor who designed your course hopes you will take advantage of the opportunity to learn about the subject. Your own objectives in taking the course could be different. You may be taking it because it fulfills some requirement for graduation or because it fits into your schedule or because it seems less objectionable than the alternative you could be taking.

In a better world, these differences between your objectives and the aims of the course would not matter. The studying you do to perform well on exams and papers would involve your learning a fair amount of the discipline. And so your grade would certify that you had indeed left the course with a more informed and thoughtful understanding of its material than you had when you entered it. In the world we must actually live in, the connection between studying a subject and studying for exams in the subject is not necessarily so clear or straightforward.

Many students manage to prepare themselves for mid-terms and finals without permanently adding to their understanding. There they sit, yellow hi-liting pens in hand, plodding through the assigned chapters. Grim-faced, they underline every declarative sentence. Then they trace and retrace their tracks, trying to commit every yellowed fact to memory. As the time of the test draws near, they choke back the first faint feeling of panic by trying to guess the likeliest questions. By such tactics they may get ready for the exam but sabotage their chance of gaining any insight into the wider themes of the course.

Life does afford worse disasters. This one, however, is remediable. And this section of *Thinking and Writing* can help. It is designed to help you do well in the course, and to help you learn the subject in its own worth. These suggestions proceed on the proposition that the easiest and most satisfying way to succeed in a course is to learn its important themes and materials.

It makes very little sense, after all, to spend your time memorizing every possible detail. You may pick up a few points on the short-answer section of the exam, but those few points are a small reward for hours of studying. And, in the meantime, your comprehension of the depths of American literature, or your sensitivity to the wonderful diversity of biological processes, is mediocre.

Studying for exams is a poor way of learning anything. Learning a subject, to the contrary, is an excellent way of preparing for exams. Grasping the larger outlines of a topic makes possible the memorizing of the facts within them: the facts that you have expected your teacher to ask. The object of this essay is to persuade you to make some changes in the way you study.

Begin by conserving your yellow pens. All that hi-liting simply lowers the resale value of the book. If you underline everything you read, you will wind up with a book of underlinings. That may bring some psychological comfort. All of that yellow does provide visible evidence that you read the material. It will not leave you with a useful guide to what to review. You have hi-lited too much, creating a democracy of facts. All authors, dates, and events are equally yellow. You need, more than anything else, some way of determining which are important.

The next step may prove harder. You will have to give up trying to learn by rote. A certain amount of memorizing may be unavoidable, but ultimately it is the enemy of understanding. That is because many people use it as an alternative to thinking. Have you ever wished there were a better way? Well, there is. Suppose you expect an examination to ask you about nineteenth-century New England authors and what their literary intentions were. You could take each writer separately and pound into your head information about Ralph Waldo Emerson's ideas, along with Nathaniel Hawthorne's and those of Henry David Thoreau. Or you could look at something that united them, their fascination with nature: the magnificent nature of the continent and the human nature that it mirrors. Then you might more easily remember Emerson's search for a source of inspiration within human nature, Hawthorne's grim sense of the wilderness within us, Thoreau's effort to cultivate his nature at the unspoiled edge of Walden Pond.

If you take care of the ideas, the facts will assemble themselves. That has to do with the way in which textbooks are written and courses taught. It also relates to how people learn.

No teacher or instructor pretends that the present state of knowledge, or any future state, can embrace all the facts of a subject. Even though scholars are always interested in finding new information, and in finding new ways of using information already known, each individual article, doctoral dissertation, monograph, textbook, or course of lectures represents hundreds and thousands of choices about what to include and what to omit. The information you actually encounter in a course, as a result, is there because the text authors or your teacher decided for some reason to include it. Usually the reason is that this particular bit of information helps explain or illustrate some pattern of behavior or thought. Focus on these patterns. They are what you should be thinking about.

In doing so, you will have the approval of learning theorists. They have found that while it is difficult for people to recall disconnected bits of data, it is comparatively easy to remember details of coherent stories.

Neither compulsive underlining nor prodigious memorization will help you to understand these patterns. What will? Rephrase the question: What does it mean to read and listen intelligently?

For most students, reading and listening are passive forms of behavior. They sit and wait to be told. Someone else, they expect, will provide the answers. Even worse is that they expect that someone else will provide the questions.

Letting your teacher or the authors of the text do your thinking for you leads to tedium. Passivity is boring. Yet people rarely blame themselves for being bored. It cannot be your own fault. You are only "taking" the course. Someone else is "giving" it, and so you look to the instructor to liven things up a touch. Maybe some audio-visuals or a bit of humor, you think, would make the course less dreary. These hopes are misplaced, for while humor is a blessed thing and audio-visuals have their place, it is the substance of the course that should interest you.

Boredom is almost always a self-inflicted wound. Students are bored because they expect the instructor always to be interesting when it is they who must themselves take an interest.

Taking an interest involves learning to read and listen actively. Intellectual activity begins with questions—your own questions directed, in the first instance, to yourself and then to your teacher. Why is it, you might wonder, that the United States is the only industrialized country without a comprehensive national system of health care? Why were New England authors drawn to the innocence or the mysterious evil of the wilderness in nature and the soul? How do rock strata yield their data to geologists?

You will not always find satisfactory answers. But you will have started to think about the meaning of the subject. And when you do, something quite desirable happens to all of those facts. They will take on life and become evidence, clues to the answers you are seeking. The questions will give you a rational basis for deciding which facts are important.

All of this leads directly to the question of how you should study for a course. It is too easy to assume that the sole reason why students are sometimes ill-prepared is that they did not spend enough time getting ready. This is a half-truth, and a dangerous one. It ignores the inefficiency of much reviewing itself.

How do you get ready for an exam? Do you get out your textbook and notes and pour over them again and again until the time runs out or the sheer boredom of it all crushes your good intentions? If so, then you have lots of company—a consolation of sorts. Available, on the other hand, is a better way.

Find a quiet and comfortable spot. Bring along a blank pad and something to write with. Then jot down, just as they occur to you, whatever items you can remember about the course. Do not rush yourself. And do not try, at this stage, to put things in order. Just sit there and scribble down whatever pops into your mind. After a while you will have quite a large and varied mix of facts. Then see how much of this you can put together. You do not need to write out whole sentences or paragraphs. An arrow or a word or two will frequently be enough. You are not, after all, going to hand in these scribbles. You are just collecting your thoughts. Do not be concerned if this process seems to be taking up some of the limited time you have to study. It will prove to be time well spent.

Now look over what you have written. Where are the gaps? You will find that you know a fair bit about the material just from your previous reading of the text and from listening in class. But some topics will still be obscure. Now you know what you should be studying. Why study what you already know? And here is the nub of the matter, for an intelligent review focuses on what you need to refresh your mind about.

You will doubtless have noticed that this strategy presupposes that you have read the textbook and taken good notes in class. Just what, you might wonder, are good notes? Many students think that the closer they come to transcribing the instructor's every word the better their notes are. They are mistaken, and for several reasons.

One is that unless you are an expert at shorthand, you will not succeed. Instead you will be frantically scrambling to catch up. At the end of class you will have a sore hand, a great deal of barely legible notes, and little if any idea of what the class was about.

Another reason not to attempt to transcribe lectures—taping them usually wastes time—is that you will spend much of your hour taking down information you either already know or can easily find in the textbook. How often do you need to see that Jefferson Davis was the president of the Confederacy?

The most important reason not to take down everything is that it prevents you from doing what you ought to be doing during class, listening intelligently. Your instructor is not simply transmitting information but also seeking to explain the principles of the discipline. It is these explanations you should be listening for, and your notes should concentrate on them. It is much easier to do this if you have read the relevant textbook chapters first. That way you will already know much of the information. And you will have some questions already in your mind, something to listen for. You can take notes sensibly. You can fill in explanations of points that had puzzled you, jot down unfamiliar facts, and devote most of your time to listening instead of writing. Your hand will not be sore; you will know what the class was about; and your notes will complement rather than duplicate what you already knew.

So far we have dealt mainly with the mechanics of studying—taking notes, reviewing for exams, and the like. Valuable as knowing the mechanics can be, the real secret to studying is learning how to think within the ultimate intentions and boundaries of the field. Biology is an attempt to understand the flow and self-articulation of life through its innumerable species and its ways of generation. History is a way of thinking about the human condition. Scholars of literature quarrel about the essence of their topic, but together they study the imagination of writers and the means by which words shapen and express that imagination. And so, as you learn the details of the subject and the ways those details relate to one another, think even more broadly what the field of study is all about. Think not only of a particular species, but of the innumerable new species that might come of its reproductive processes; consider both the specific causes of the Civil War and the universal motives of pride and greed and loyalty that found an occasion then; reflect not solely on the effect of nature on the New England mind but on the task of all writers who seek the exact phrase to speak their mind.

HOW TO TAKE EXAMS

In the best of worlds examinations would hold no terrors. You would be so well prepared that no question, no matter how tricky or obscure, could shake your serene confidence. In the real world, it seems, preparation is always less than complete. "Of course," you say to yourself, "I should have studied more. But I did not. Now what?" This section will not tell you how to get A's without study, but it will suggest some practical steps that will help you earn the highest grade compatible with what you do know.

Before you begin answering any of the essay portion of the exam, look over the entire essay section. It is impossible to budget your time sensibly until you know what the whole exam looks like. And if you fail to allow enough time for each question, two things—both bad—are likely to happen. You may have to leave some questions out, including perhaps some you might have answered very effectively. How often have you muttered: "I really knew that one"? The other unhappy consequence is that you may have to rush through the last part of the exam, including questions you could have answered very well if you had left more time.

How do you budget your time effectively? The idea, after all, is to make sure that you have enough time to answer fully all the questions you do know. So the best plan is also the simplest. Answer those questions first.

Answering question #7 before #4 may seem odd at first, but you will soon enough get used to it. And you will find that, if you still run out of time, you at least have the satisfaction of knowing you are rushing through questions you could not have answered very well anyway. You will have guaranteed that you will receive the maximum credit for what you do know. Answering questions in the order of your knowledge has an immediate psychological advantage too. Most students are at least a little tense before an exam. If you answer the first several questions well, that tension will likely go away. As you relax, you will find it easier to remember names, dates, and other bits of information. If you get off to a shaky start, a simple case of pre-exam jitters can become full-scale panic. Should that happen, you may have trouble remembering your own phone number.

Let us suppose you have gotten through everything you think you know on the exam and still have some time left. What should you do? You can now try to pick up a few extra points with some judicious guessing. Trying to guess with essay questions is of little use. In all probability you will write something so vague that you will not get any credit for it anyway. You should try instead to score on the short answer section.

Some types of questions were made for shrewd guesswork. Matching columns are ideal. A process of elimination will often tell you what the answer has to be. Multiple choice questions are almost as good. Here too you can eliminate some of the possibilities. Most teachers feel obliged to give you a choice of four or five possible answers, but find it hard to come up with more than three that are plausible. So you can normally count on being able to recognize the one or two that are there just as padding. Once you have narrowed the choices to two or three, you are ready to make your educated guess. Always play your hunches, however vague. Your hunch is based on something you heard or read even if you cannot remember what it is. So go with it. Do not take your time. If you cannot think of the answer, just pick one and have done with it. Try to avoid changing answers. A number of studies show that you are more likely to change a right answer than to correct a wrong one.

Identifications are the type of short-answer question most resistant to guesswork. Don't spend much time on questions for which you have little idea of an answer, but try to come up with something better than a slapdash hunch. (This does not contradict the advice about playing hunches on multiple-choice questions. Such questions offer alternatives, one of which may tickle your memory.) You want the exam as a whole to convey what you do know. Supplying a mass of misinformation usually creates a presumption that you do not know what you are talking about even on those sections of the exam for which you really do. So be careful about wild guesses. Be prepared to present your instructor with a solid assemblage of good factual answers that will indicate that while you have achieved a critical understanding of the themes of the course, you have also respected the facts to which those themes speak.

These suggestions are not substitutes for studying. They may, however, help you get the most out of what you know. They may, that is, make the difference between a mediocre and a good grade.

HOW TO WRITE BOOK REVIEWS

One goal of book reviews is to set forth clearly and succinctly who would benefit from reading the work in question. It follows that a good review indicates the scope of the book, identifies its point of view, summarizes its main conclusions, evaluates its use of evidence, and—where possible—compares the book with others on the subject.

You have probably written book reviews in high school or in other college courses. You may then be in danger of approaching this kind of assignment with a false sense of security. It sounds easy, after all, to write an essay of five hundred words or so. And you have written lots of other reviews. But did those other reviews concentrate clearly on the questions a good review must address? If they did not, your previous experience is not going to prove especially helpful. You may even have developed some bad habits.

Easily the worst habit is that of summarizing not the book's argument but its contents. Let us suppose you are reviewing a biography of Ernest Hemingway. The temptation is to write about Hemingway rather than about the book. This is a path to disaster. Hemingway had an eventful but widely known career. You are not, in all probability, going to find that much that is fresh or interesting to say about him. Meanwhile you have ignored your primary responsibility, which is to tell the reader what this study has to say that is fresh or interesting.

So you need to remind yourself as forcefully as possible that your job is to review the book and not the subject of the book. Does the book fix narrowly on Hemingway or does it also go into the literary circle to which he belonged? Is the author sympathetic to him? Does the writer attempt to psychoanalyze him or stick to questions of his style and themes? Is the book in firm command of the available evidence (this requires you to read the footnotes)? Does the author have something new to say about Hemingway and his times? If so, how well documented is this new interpretation?

You should generally not comment on whether you enjoyed the book. That is undoubtedly an important consideration for you, but it is of little interest to anyone else. There are occasions when you need to suffer in silence. This is one of them.

HOW TO SELECT A TERM PAPER TOPIC

Doing research, as you may already have had occasion to learn, is hard work. It is sometimes boring. Typically it involves long periods of going through material that is not what you were looking for and is not particularly interesting. It also involves taking detailed and careful notes, many of which you will never use. These are the dues you must pay if you are ever to earn the excitement that comes when you finally find the missing piece of evidence and make sense of things.

Not everything about doing research is boring. Aside from the indescribable sensation of actually finding out what you wanted to know are occasional happy accidents when you stumble across something that while not relevant to your research nonetheless pricks your imagination. Many a scholar studying an old political campaign has read up on the pennant races or fashions or radio listings for that year. These are, as one scholar puts it, oases in the desert of evidence. But, as he quickly adds, no one crosses the desert just to get to the oasis. The truth of the matter is that you have to have a good reason for getting to the other side. This means a topic you are genuinely interested in.

The point cannot be overemphasized. If you have a question you really want to answer, you will find it much easier to endure the tedium of turning all those pages. You will have a motive for taking good notes and for keeping your facts straight. If you are not interested in your topic, you are going to be constantly tempted to take shortcuts. And even if you resist temptation, you will find it hard to think seriously about what you do find.

So the topic has to interest you. That, you may be thinking, is easy to say. But what if your interest in the subject is less than compelling? Are you then going to be stuck with some topic you could care little about? The answer is No. No, that is, unless it turns out that you have no curiosity about anything at all; and if that is the case, you are probably dead already. Anything that can be examined chronologically is fair game for the historian. Histories exist of sports and of sciences, of sexual practices and jokes about them, of work and of recreation. Suppose the course is in literature. Can you find no poem, no novel, no body of literary criticism that has anything you want to talk about? Is sociology, or politics, or anthropology a dry creek? Surely your imagination can find a topic on which you and your instructor will agree. This being true, if you wind up writing on some question you are not passionately concerned with answering, you alone are at fault.

Once you have such a topic you need to find ways of defining it so that you can write an intelligent essay. "The Automobile in American Life" could serve as the subject for a very long book. It is not going to work as a subject for a term paper. You could not possibly search out so vast a topic in the time you have to work with. And your paper, however long, is not going to be of book length, so you would be stuck with trying to compress an immense amount of information into a brief essay. You need to fix on some element of the general topic that you can intelligently treat in the space and time you have to work with.

Students usually look at this problem backwards. They complain about how long their papers have to be. They should complain about how short they have to be. Space is a luxury you normally cannot afford. If you have done a fair amount of research on an interesting topic, your problem is going to be one of finding a way of getting into your paper all you have to say. Writing consists of choices about what you want to say. And if you have done your work properly, the hard choices involve deciding what to leave out.

"Fair enough," you may be thinking, "but I do not want to get stuck investigating some minute bit of trivia, the 'gear shift level from 1940 to 1953,' for example. I want to study the automobile in American life." Here we come to the core of the matter. Your topic must be narrowly defined so that you can do it justice, but it must also speak to the broad question that interested you in the first place. The trick is to decide just what it is about your topic—cars in this instance—that really interests you. Cars are means of transportation, of course, but they are also status symbols, examples of technology, and much else. Because of the automobile, cities and suburbs are designed in ways very different from how they were when people traveled by trolley or train. The automobile has dictated even teenage dating patterns. Having a driver's license, and regular access to a car, has become for some teenagers an obsession.

The point is that you have to think about your topic and then decide what within it to examine. If you end up doing a treatise on differing methods of changing tires, you are your own enemy. You could have been studying sex and sexism in automobile advertising.

HOW TO LOCATE MATERIAL

Once you have worked up an interesting and practical topic for your term paper, you are ready to begin your research. For many students this means ambling over to the library and poking around in the computer catalog. This may not be the best way to begin. The librarians who catalog the library's holdings, while skilled professionals, cannot possibly anticipate the needs of every individual student. So they catalog books by their main subject headings and then include obvious cross-references. But much of what you need may not be obvious. So, for example, if you are interested in the causes of the Civil War, you will have no trouble finding under "U.S. History, Civil War" a title such as Kenneth Stampp's *And the War Came.* But will you find Roy Nichol's *Disruption of the American*

Democracy? Your subject, however, may have a general guide, such as the *Harvard Guide to American History*. In that case, draw titles from it.

Now you have the beginnings of a decent bibliography. Your next act should be to introduce yourself to the research librarian. This person's specialty is helping people look for information. Yet many students never consult with a librarian. Do not pass up an opportunity to make your work easier. Often a librarian can point you to more specialized bibliographical guides, show you where to learn of the most recent books and articles, and help you refine your topic by indicating what questions are easiest to get information on.

You now have a reasonably extensive set of cards. And you can now safely consult the card catalog to see which of these titles your library has. Prepare yourself for some disappointments. Even good undergraduate libraries will not have everything you need. They will have some (unless your library is very weak or your topic esoteric). Almost all college libraries participate in the interlibrary loan system. This system, which the library staff will gladly explain to you, permits you to get virtually any title you could wish for. The only catch is that you must give the library enough lead time. For books and articles that are not especially rare this normally means from a day or two to two weeks.

HOW TO TAKE NOTES

Sifting through the material you have found, you will need to take careful notes. As you do, you should write down on a notecard each piece of information you believe might prove relevant. For each piece of information you also will have to specify the full source.

Following these two bits of advice will save you much time and trouble. Finding information in your sources is trouble enough. You do not want to have to find it all over again when you sit down to write your paper. But this is often just what students have to do because they failed to write down some bit of data (which, perhaps, seemed only marginally important at the time) or took all of their notes on loose leaf paper and now must search through every page to find this one fact. It is far easier, over the long run, to have a separate card for each piece or group of closely related pieces of information. Tell yourself that you are the last of the big time spenders and can afford to use up index cards as though they were blank pieces of paper, which is what they are.

The general rule is that in compiling your research notes you should take extra care so that the actual writing will be as trouble-free as possible. It follows that you should take lots of notes. Do not try to determine in advance whether you are going to use a particular bit of data. Always give yourself the margin of safety. Similarly, do not try to decide in advance whether you will quote the source exactly or simply paraphrase it. If you take down the exact words, you can always decide to make the idea your own by qualifying it in various ways and putting it in your own words.

WRITING TERM PAPERS AND OTHER ESSAYS

You have no doubt already learned that next to mastery of the subject matter nothing is more important for earning good grades than effective writing. You surely know people who despite weak study habits get high grades. The reason may be their ability to write well.

Students who are not among that relatively small group who write well sometimes think it unfair that writing skills should count so heavily. The course, some complain, is in biology, or geology, or European literature, and not expository writing, and so their prose should not influence their grade. But teachers continue to believe that the ability clearly and forcefully to express what you know is an indispensable measure of how well you have learned the subject. Writing well is an invaluable skill, and not only in college. Many of the most desirable jobs involve writing: correspondence, reports, memoranda. The writing will never stop.

No matter how poorly you write, if you can speak English effectively you can learn to write it effectively. It is simply a matter of expressing your ideas clearly. This you can learn to do. It requires not genius but merely patience and practice.

Charity, St. Paul said, is the chief of all the virtues. In expository prose, however, the chief virtue is clarity. And like charity, it covers a multitude of sins. If your sentences, however homely, are clear, they will receive a sympathetic reading.

It has perhaps crossed your mind that on some occasions you are not very eager to get to the point. Sometimes you may not be sure just what the point is. Sometimes you do know, but are not convinced that your point is a very good one. At such times, a little obfuscation may seem a better idea than clarity. It is not. Nothing is more troubling than reading a paper in which the author tried to hedge bets or fudge ideas. The very worst thing you can do is leave it up to your reader to decide what you are trying to say. So no matter how weak your ideas seem to you, set them forth clearly. Something is always better than nothing. Most teachers are interested in helping students. It is much easier to help you if your instructor can figure out what you were trying to say.

And teachers delight in watching students improve. The reason is obvious: They see it as proof that they are doing a good job. They take special pleasure in the progress of students who start off poorly but steadily get better over the course of the semester. You can do a lot worse than be one of those students.

I urge you, then, to give close attention to the advice this manual has offered on good writing. If you have the energy, learn to write gracefully. But in any event, write clearly.

WHEN AND HOW TO USE FOOTNOTES

Many students apparently believe that the only thing worse than having to read footnotes is having to write them. It is easy to understand why they feel that way, but they are making much ado about very little. Footnotes inform the reader where the information in the body of the paper can be found. That is the substance of the matter.

So when should you use a footnote? One occasion is when you are referring to someone's exact words whether by direct quotation or by paraphrase. (If your paper does not require footnotes, you need only mention the author's name at the time you quote.) The other is when you are referring to some bit of information that is not already well known or is someone's interpretation of the facts. How, you might wonder, can you tell whether or not something is already well known? A simple rule is that nothing you can find in a standard textbook needs to be footnoted. Hence, for example, you do not have to footnote that George Washington was the first President of the United States. You may need to footnote an exact quotation from his "Farewell Address." You do not need to footnote that F. Scott

Fitzgerald was the author of *The Great Gatsby*. If you are in doubt about a particular case, you still have two steps open to you. One is to ask your instructor, the reader you are seeking to inform in the first place. The other, if you find it impracticable to reach your teacher, is to use the footnote. Having an unnecessary footnote is a minor flaw. Not having a necessary one is a serious omission. So you can simply err on the safe side.

Now that you know when to use footnotes, you can consider the matter of how to use them. Several formats are in common use. Simply ask your instructor which one is preferred. If your teacher has no preference, invest in the inexpensive Modern Language Association (MLA) style sheet. It is brief, clearly written, reliable, and cheap. It is very unlikely you will encounter a question it will not answer.

WHAT TO INCLUDE IN YOUR BIBLIOGRAPHY

Early in your research you compiled a list of possible sources. The temptation is to type out a bibliography from those cards. This is fine provided that you actually used all of those sources. Your bibliography should include all the sources you consulted and only those sources. So even though you have all sorts of cards, and even though your bibliography would look far more authoritative if you included sources you looked up but did not use, do not do so. It is most unlikely that padding your bibliography will impress.

A WORD ABOUT PLAGIARISM AND ORIGINALITY

Plagiarism is the act of claiming another's work as your own. It is about as serious an academic offense as you can commit. Many colleges require teachers to report all instances of plagiarism, and while the punishment can vary, it is always stiff. And of all the various ways of cheating, teachers find plagiarism the easiest to detect.

Some students plagiarize without realizing that this is what they are doing. They quote from a book or article without so indicating by quotation marks or citing the author and the work, or they paraphrase a passage without proper acknowledgment. They have unintentionally passed off someone else's work as their own. Sometimes this results in nothing worse than a private lecture from the instructor on the necessity of correctly attributing all information. Even so it is embarrassing, and it creates the impression that you do not know what you are doing. So be sure you indicate the sources not only of your information but also of the interpretations or ideas you include in your papers.

Teachers will often tell their students that their papers should be original. Scholars use this word in a somewhat different sense from what you might expect. In ordinary speech something is original if it is the first of its kind or the only one of its kind. Scholars mean something less dramatic. We refer to research as "original" if the researcher did the work. We do not mean that the conclusions have never been reached before or that no one else has ever used the same source materials. The way you put together familiar information and ideas may be original.

Do not hesitate to make use of ideas from other scholars. No one with any sense expects beginning students to make startling discoveries or to develop radically new perspectives. It is, accordingly, perfectly legitimate for you to use other people's insights. The only hitch is that you must always acknowledge where they came from.

Appendix I

VOCABULARY

The best way to expand your vocabulary is to read widely. While memorizing obscure words has little point, it is of course helpful to know common ones familiar to educated people. This list gives pronunciation within parentheses, and the accent goes on the syllable in capital letters.

abate *(a-BATE), verb*
To diminish or reduce in intensity

abdicate *(AB-di-kate), verb*
To relinquish a position of high authority

aberration *(ab-a-RAY-shun), noun*
Deviation from customary behavior

abet *(a-BET), verb*
To encourage or aid a plan of action

abhorrent *(ab-HOR-ent), adjective*
Detestable or contemptible

abide *(a-BIDE), verb*
To stay somewhere a long time

abject *(AB-jekt), adjective*
Downcast, disheartened

abjure *(ab-JUR), verb*
To renounce a former commitment

abortive *(a-BOR-tive), adjective*
Stopped or failed before the conclusion

abrade *(a-BRADE), verb*
To wear away

abrogate *(AB-ro-gate), verb*
To abolish or cancel a treaty, law, or other official commitment

abscond *(ab-SKOND), verb*
To leave quickly and secretly for the purpose of avoiding prosecution for wrongdoing

absolve *(ab-ZOLV), verb*
To hold someone blameless of an immoral act

abstemious *(ab-STEE-me-us), adjective*
Living austerely, abstaining from pleasures

abstinence *(AB-ste-nence), noun*
Rejection of some particular need or pleasure

abstruse *(ab-STRUCE), adjective*
Complicated, dense

accede *(ak-SEED), verb*
To consent

accolade *(AK-uh-lade), noun*
A token of praise

accrue *(a-CRUE), verb*
To gain as an increase or advantage

acquiescence *(ak-wee-ESS-unce), noun*
Passive agreement

acrid *(AK-rid), adjective*
Harsh in smell or taste

acrimonious *(ak-ri-MO-nee-us), adjective*
Bittter, sharp in a verbal exchange

acumen *(a-CUE-men), noun*
Keen judgment

ad hoc *(ad HOK), adjective*
Formed for a specific purpose

ad infinitum *(ad in-fi-NIGH-tum), adjective*
Endlessly, to infinity

adage *(AD-ij), noun*
A pithy saying (don't say "old adage")

adamant *(AD-uh-mant), adjective*
Holding stubbornly to a position

adept *(a-DEPT), adjective*
Skilled, proficient

adroit *(a-DROIT), adjective*
Nimble, adept

affinity *(a-FIN-ih-tee), noun*
Natural attraction to something

aggravate *(AG-gra-vayt), verb*
To make larger a bad condition

alacrity *(a-LACK-rih-tee), noun*
Quickness and eagerness in embrace of a project

albatross *(AL-ba-tross), noun*
A burden, impediment

allay *(a-LAY), verb*
To calm, ease a fear, doubt, or pain

allude *(a-LOOD), verb*
To refer to in passing

altruism *(AL-troo-ihz-um), noun*
Selfless action for the betterment of others

ambivalent *(am-BIV-uh-lent), adjective*
Uncertain, undecided in the face of possibilities

ameliorate *(a-MEEL-oh-rate), verb*
To make better

amoral *(ay-MOR-al), adjective*
Acting or thinking without any consideration of right or wrong

anachronism *(a-NAK-roh-niz-um), adjective*
Placing an event earlier or later than it could actually have happened

anathema *(a-NATH-eh-muh), noun*
A denunciation or the person or thing denouced

ancillary *(AN-se-lare-ree), adjective*
Secondary, supplementary

anomaly *(a-NOM-a-lee), noun*
A divergence from expectation

antebellum *(an-tee-BELL-uhm), adjective*
Preceding a war, specifically the American Civil War

antiquity *(an-TIK-wi-tee), noun*
Ancient times

apocalyptic *(a-pok-uh-LIP-tic), adjective*
So destructive as to seem the end of the world

apocryphal *(a-POK-ri-fal), adjective*
Of doubtful truth: used of stories

apropos *(ap-roh-POE), adjective*
Relevant to a subject

ascetic *(a-SET-ik), adjective*
Practicing self-denial

ascribe *(a-SKRYBE), verb*
To attribute

assiduous *(a-SID-jue-us), adjective*
Relentless in attention, constant in labor

belated *(bee-LAY-ted), adjective*
Late, past due

beleaguered *(bee-LEEG-erd), adjective*
Embattled

belie *(bee-LYE), verb*
To indicate the opposite of a claim or apparent fact

belligerent *(bih-LIJ-er-ent), adjective*
Eager to fight

bemused *(bee-MYUZD), adjective*
Lost in reflection

bequeath *(be-QUEETH), verb*
To bestow in a will

bereaved *(bih-REEVD), adjective*
In a state of mourning for the loss of someone close

beseech *(bih-SEECH), verb*
To entreat, implore

bestow *(bih-STOW), verb*
To confer an award, honor, or gift

bête noire *(bett NWAHR), noun*
Something that a person especially detests or fears

bigamy *(BIG-a-mee), noun*
The crime of taking marriage vows but remaining legally married to someone else

bilateral *(bye-LAT-er-al), adjective*
Involving or pertaining to both parties to a treaty or other contract

bilk *(bilk), verb*
To swindle or cheat

binary *(BYE-nair-ee), adjective*
Of or pertaining to two

biogenesis *(bye-oh-JEN-ih-siss), noun*
The process of life's arising from other living things

bipolar *(bye-POE-lar), adjective*
Possessing two poles; marked by opposed extremes

blasé *(blah-ZAY), adjective*
Appearing bored or unimpressed with life or surroundings

blather *(BLATH-er), verb*
To babble or talk ridiculously

blithe *(blithe), adjective*
Carefree, high-spirited

bohemian *(bo-HEE-mee-an), adjective*
Unconventional, free of the restraints of mainstream society: associated especially with artists

bombast *(BOM-bast), noun*
Overblown or pompous talk or writing

bona fide *(BOE-na fyde), adjective*
Genuine

boorish *(BOOR-ish), adjective*
Lacking manners and civility

brash *(brash), adjective*
Hasty, impetuous

brevity *(BREV-ih-tee), noun*
Briefness

brusque *(brusk), adjective*
Abrupt, curt

calvary *(CAL-va-ree), noun*
The hill on which Christ was crucified; an occasion of suffering in which virtue is tested or a truth is revealed

canard *(ka-NARD), noun*
An untrue story, especially to discredit a person, idea, or thing

candor *(KAN-duhr), noun*
Frankness, openness

capacious *(kuh-PAY-shus), adjective*
Spacious, encompassing a large area or quantity

capricious *(kuh-PREE-shuss), adjective*
Quick to make changes in plans or ideas

captious *(KAP-shuss), adjective*
Quick to find fault

cardinal *(KAR-dih-nal), adjective*
Of primary importance, vital

caricature *(KARE-ihk-a-chure), noun*
An exaggerated representation

carpe diem *(KAR-pay DEE-uhm), noun*
Latin for "seize the day": take meaning and pleasure from whatever the day or the moment offers

carte blanche *(kart blonsh), noun*
Unrestricted freedom to act

catch-22 *(KATCH-twen-tee-too), noun*
A threatening situation in which each of the

apparently differing means of escape will lead to the same ill result

catharsis *(ka-THAR-siss), noun*
A purging of the emotions that results in clarity and health

caustic *(KOSS-tick), adjective*
Searingly critical and sarcastic

cavalier *(KAV-a-leer), adjective*
Possessing a haughty and dismissive attitude

cavalry *(CAV-al-ree), noun*
A unit of soldiers on horseback

celerity *(seh-LAIR-ih-tee), noun*
Swiftness of action or movement

celibacy *(SELL-ih-bus-see), noun*
Abstaining from sexual activity

charismatic *(kare-ihz-MAT-ik), adjective*
Possessing a power to inspire or lead

charlatan *(SHAR-luh-tunn), noun*
A fake, humbug

chimerical *(kih-MARE-ih-cal), adjective*
Fanciful, unreal

circumlocution *(sir-kum-lo-CUE-shun), noun*
Wordy and indirect argument, explanation, or description

citadel *(SIT-a-del), noun*
A stronghold

clandestine *(klan-DESS-tin), adjective*
Hidden, secreted

clemency *(KLEM-uhn-see), noun*
Mercy toward a wrongdoer or an enemy

coalesce *(ko-uh-LESS), verb*
To unite into a single whole

cogent *(KOE-jent), adjective*
Tightly reasoned or phrased and therefore persuasive

colloquial *(kuh-LO-kwee-ul), adjective*
Belonging to a class of words and phrases that are informal, and perhaps regional in origin, but without being slang

commensurate *(kuh-MEN-sir-it), adjective*
Being of the same measure in size, strength, importance, or conduct

concurrence *(kun-KER-rence), noun*
Agreement or some other coming together

confluence *(KON-flu-ence), noun*
A flowing together of streams of water or of events or actions

congenital *(kun-JEN-it-ul), adjective*
Originating in biological conception

conjecture *(kun-JEK-shur), noun*
Speculation based on incomplete data

consanguineous *(con-san-GWIN-ee-us), adjective*
Related by blood

consecrate *(KON-si-krate), verb*
To dedicate to divine service or some grand objective

consternation *(kon-ster-NAY-shun), noun*
Confused amazement

consummate *(KON-sum-mate), verb*
To complete, bring to a conclusion

contrition *(kun-TRISH-un), noun*
Remorse for a sin, accompanied by a resolve to do better

convivial *(kun-VIV-ee-ul), adjective*
Amiable, especially in a festive social setting

convocation *(kon-vo-KAY-shun), noun*
An assembly of people called together

convoluted *(kon-vuh-LOO-tid), adjective*
Complicated and twisted

copious *(KO-pee-us), adjective*
Having an abundance of any desirable thing

covenant *(KUH-vuh-nent), noun*
A solemn, formal agreement

culpable *(KUL-pa-bl), adjective*
Guilty

cupidity *(kyu-PID-ih-tee), noun*
Greed

dank *(dank), adjective*
Damp and chilly

debacle *(dih-BA-kl), noun*
The total collapse of a large project

debonair *(deb-uh-NAIR), adjective*
Suave, sophisticated

decadence *(DEK-a-dunce), noun*
A state of decline in virtue and standards: used of a whole nation, segment of society, or civilization

decorum *(dih-COR-um), noun*
Propriety, dignified conduct

decrepit *(dih-KREP-it), adjective*
Enfeebled, as by advanced age

deduce *(dih-DUSE), verb*
To reason from a premise that dictates how to think about particulars

deescalate *(dee-ES-kuh-late), verb*
To diminish: used of the possibilities or ingredients of conflict

defamation *(def-uh-MAY-shun), noun*
False, baseless attack on a person's or group's reputation

deference *(DEF-er-ence), noun*
Giving respect or yielding to the judgment of a more authoritative person

degenerate *(dih-JEN-er-it), adjective*
Descended to a lower state

déjà vu *(day-zhuh VOO), noun*
The sense of having experienced a present event at some time in the past

deify *(DEE-ih-fy), verb*
To elevate to the level of divinity

deleterious *(del-i-TEER-ee-us), adjective*
Harmful, particularly to health, morals, or well-being

demagogue *(DEM-a-gog), noun*
An individual (usually a politician or other leader) who gains power by appealing to emotions and passions of the people

demarcate *(dee-MAR-kate), verb*
To establish boundaries

depravity *(dih-PRAV-ih-tee), noun*
Deep corruption

deprecate *(DEP-ri-kate), verb*
To express disapproval or belittle

desideratum *(di-sid-uh-RAH-tum), noun*
A thing to be desired

despotism *(DESS-po-tiz-um), noun*
Authoritarian rule by a despot

desultory *(DE-sul-to-ree), adjective*
Failing to work steadily toward the accomplishment of a project

diatribe *(DIE-uh-tribe), noun*
Bitter denunciation

dichotomy *(die-KOT-uh-me), noun*
Division into two contrasting parts

diffident *(DIFF-ih-dent), adjective*
Unassertive, shy

dilatory *(DIL-uh-tore-ee), adjective*
Tending to delay

dilettante *(DIL-eh-tont), noun*
A person who is interested in some subject but fails to grasp it in a serious, rigorous way

disdain *(diss-DANE), verb*
To treat contemptuously

disingenuous *(diss-in-JEN-yoo-uss), adjective*
Deliberately refraining from revealing the full truth, taking on a false air of innocent honesty

disparity *(dis-PARE-ih-tee), noun*
Nonequivalence, inequality among people or things with something in common

dissonance *(DISS-uh-nunce), noun*
An inharmonious combination of sounds

dissuade *(diss-SWADE), noun*
To persuade someone not to take a certain course

diurnal *(dye-UHR-nal), adjective*
Happening during daytime or every day

docile *(DOSS-il), adjective*
Easily led

dogmatic *(dog-MAT-ik), adjective*
Adhering rigidly to a belief

dossier *(DOSS-ee-ay), noun*
Documents offering detailed information on an individual or a matter

droll *(drole), adjective*
Wryly amusing

echelon *(ESH-uh-lon), noun*
A level of command; a formation of troops or military vehicles

eclectic *(ek-LEK-tic), adjective*
Made up of a variety of styles, philosophies, or religions

ecumenical *(ek-yu-MEN-ih-kul), adjective*
Universal: used especially of attempts to promote unity among Christians

effrontery *(ih-FRON-ter-ee), noun*
Deliberately ill-mannered and offensive boldness

egregious *(ih-GREE-juss), adjective*
Glaringly or otherwise bad

elusive *(ee-LOO-siv), adjective*
Difficult to catch or comprehend

embodiment *(em-BOD-ee-ment), noun*
The rendering of an idea into concrete form

emeritus *(ih-MARE-ih-tuss), adjective*
Of someone who has retired but still holds an honorary title

empathize *(EM-puh-thyz), verb*
To feel another's emotions

en masse *(on MASS), adverb*
Gathered together in one group

ennui *(on-WEE), noun*
Boredom accompanied by a sense of drift and purposelessness

equanimity *(ee-kwa-NIM-ih-tee), noun*
Even-temperedness, especially in the midst of distubing events

ersatz *(AIR-sats), noun*
Not the real thing

esoteric *(ess-oh-TARE-ik), adjective*
Comprehensible only to a small, restricted group

exacerbate *(ig-ZASS-ur-bate), verb*
To worsen

expeditious *(ek-spe-DISH-uss), adjective*
Speedy and efficient

expletive *(EK-splih-tive), noun*
An exclamation or profane oath

extenuate *(ik-STEN-yoo-ate), verb*
To make a wrong less serious or to find reason to see it as less serious

facetious *(fuh-SEE-shuss), adjective*
Lightly funny: used especially of a remark that does not treat a situation as seriously as needed

fait accompli *(FATE uh-com-PLEE), noun*
Something that has already been finished: used especially of a project completed before it could be stopped

fallacious *(fuh-LAY-shuss), adjective*
Containing a logical error

fastidious *(fa-STID-ee-uss), adjective*
Attentive to detail, meticulous; repelled by lack of neatness

fetid *(FET-id), adjective*
Stinking

fiasco *(fee-ASS-koe), noun*
An utter failure

flim-flam *(FLIM-flam), noun*
A swindle

flippant *(FLIP-punt), adjective*
Lightly disregarding decorum, feelings, or the seriousness of something

formidable *(FOR-mih-duh-bl), adjective*
Inspiring fear or respect

furtive *(FUR-tiv), adjective*
Stealthy, acting hiddenly

gainsay *(GANE-say), verb*
To declare false, contradict

gamut *(GAM-ut), noun*
The full range or extent

genteel *(jen-TEEL), adjective*
Refined

gentry *(JEN-tree), noun*
The class just below the nobility

goad *(goad), verb*
To prod with a stick; to taunt someone into doing something

gratuitous *(gra-TOO-ih-tuss), adjective*
Unnecessary and freely given

guile *(gile), noun*
Cunning, clever deceit

hackneyed *(HAK-need), adjective*
Employed of sayings that have lost their freshness

halcyon *(HAL-see-on), noun*
Tranquility and joyfulness: implies a dream-like distance from reality

hapless *(HAP-liss), adjective*
Luckless, unfortunate

harbinger *(HAR-bin-jur), noun*
Something that indicates the coming of an event

hardtack *(HARD-tak), noun*
A hard biscuit once common in military rations

hegemony *(he-JEM-uh-nee), noun*
Predominant power and influence

hiatus *(hie-AY-tuss), noun*
An interruption that breaks the continuity of a project

hubris *(HYOO-briss), noun*
Excessive pride that leads to a disastrous course

hyperbole *(hie-PUR-boh-lee), noun*
Overstatement, exaggeration

illicit *(ih-LISS-it), adjective*
Illegal or morally unjustifiable

imbibe *(im-BIBE), verb*
To drink: often used figuratively, as in imbibing knowledge

imbroglio *(im-BROA-lee-o), noun*
A confused situation

impasse *(IM-pass), noun*
A situation with no solution or escape

impeccable *(im-PECK-uh-bl), adjective*
Flawless, virtually perfect

imperative *(im-PAIR-uh-tiv), adjective*
Essential, necessary, commanded by the situation

imperious *(im-PEER-ee-us), adjective*
Haughtily commanding

impugn *(im-PYOON), verb*
To question someone's virtues or motives

impunity *(im-PYOO-nih-tee), noun*
Freedom from punishment

inadvertent *(in-ad-VER-tnt), adjective*
Happening in a moment of forgetfulness or inattention

inane *(in-ANE), adjective*
Pointless and silly

incarnate *(in-KAR-nat), adjective*
Embodied

inception *(in-SEP-shun), noun*
Beginning

incessant *(in-SESS-unt), adjective*
Continuous

incorrigible *(in-KORE-ij-uh-bl), adjective*
Incapable of being reformed

indefatigable *(in-di-FAT-ih-ga-bl), adjective*
Tireless

indolent *(IN-do-lnt), adjective*
Lazy

infrastructure *(IN-fruh-struk-chur), noun*
The physical and technological framework of a country, region, or particular operation:

used especially of transport and communications

innate *(ih-NATE), adjective*
Inborn, inherent

innocuous *(ih-NOK-yoo-us), adjective*
Harmless

insipid *(in-SIP-id), adjective*
Lacking in color, flow, and vigor

intransigent *(in-TRAN-si-jent), adjective*
Unyielding in opinion or resolve

intrepid *(in-TREP-id), adjective*
Stubbornly courageous

jejune *(ji-JOON), adjective*
Childish, lacking mature judgment

jingoistic *(jin-go-ISS-tik), adjective*
Belligerently nationalistic

jocular *(JOK-yoo-lur), adjective*
Joking in manner

jurisprudence *(jur-iss-PROO-dence), noun*
The science of law

juxtapose *(JUK-sta-pose), verb*
To place side by side, especially for comparison

kinetic *(kih-NET-ik), adjective*
Pertaining to motion

laconic *(la-KON-ik), adjective*
Speaking briefly, dryly, and to the point

languid *(LANG-gwid), adjective*
Listless, lacking vitality

lethargic *(la-THAR-jik), adjective*
Sluggish, inactive

litany *(LIT-uh-nee), noun*
A long repetitive account, especially if listing wrongs suffered

litigious *(lih-TIJ-us), adjective*
Inclined to engage in lawsuits

ludicrous *(LOO-dih-kruss), adjective*
Absurd

lugubrious *(loo-GOO-bree-us), adjective*
Mournful in manner or appearance

machination *(mak-ih-NAY-shun), noun*
A conniving plot

macrocosm *(MAK-roh-koz-um), noun*
Wholeness that contains within it smaller versions of itself

magnate *(MAG-nayt), noun*
An industrial leader

malady *(MAL-uh-dee), noun*
An illness

malinger *(ma-LING-ger), verb*
To avoid work by making excuses

martial *(MAR-shill), adjective*
Of war or the military

matriarch *(MAY-tree-ark), noun*
A woman who presides over a family or group

meander *(mee-AN-der), verb*
To follow a turning and winding path

mellifluous *(mih-LIF-loo-us), adjective*
Flowing sweetly and smoothly

mendacious *(men-DAY-shuss), adjective*
Lying, false

mentor *(MEN-tor), noun*
A counselor or teacher

mesmerize *(MEZ-mer-ize), verb*
To hypnotize, capture the mind and emotions of people so that their judgment is suspended

microcosm *(MY-kro-koz-um), noun*
A smaller version of a whole

millenium *(mih-LEN-ee-um), noun*
A period of one thousand years, or the last

moment of that time; a time of peace, justice, and happiness

mitigate *(MIH-tih-gate), verb*
To lessen a pain or sorrow

mollify *(MOL-ih-fy), verb*
To allay, calm an anger

monograph *(MON-uh-graff), noun*
A scholarly work on a specific topic

mundane *(mun-DANE), adjective*
Ordinary, everyday

munificent *(myoo-NIF-ih-sent), adjective*
Generous

myriad *(MEER-ee-ad), adjective*
Innumerable or great in number

napalm *(NAY-pom), noun*
Burning jellylike substance used in war

narcissistic *(nar-sis-SIS-tik), adjective*
Obsessed by self-love

nascent *(NAY-sent), adjective*
Beginning to develop or emerge

nebulous *(NEB-yoo-luss), adjective*
Cloudlike, vague

nefarious *(nih-FARE-ee-us), adjective*
Evil, sinister

nemesis *(NEM-i-sis), noun*
An unconquerable enemy who defines the life and limits of an individual

neolithic *(nee-o-LITH-ik), adjective*
Pertaining to the later part of the Stone Age

neophyte *(NEE-ih-fite), noun*
A recent convert; a beginner at some difficult skill or learning

nepotism *(NEP-ih-tiz-um), noun*
Favoritism toward relatives in professional matters

nether *(NETH-er), adjective*
Pertaining to regions dark and beneath the surface

neurology *(noo-ROL-oh-gee), noun*
The study of the nervous system and its diseases

nexus *(NEK-sus), noun*
A linkage or connection

nirvana *(nir-VAH-nah), noun*
A state of spiritual perfection and freedom from needs and cravings

noblesse oblige *(no-BLESS oh-BLEEZH), noun*
Benevolence befitting high station

nocturnal *(nok-TUR-nal), adjective*
Pertaining to night

nonpareil *(non-pa-RELL), noun*
A person without equal

obsolescence *(ob-soh-LESS-unce), noun*
Condition of being outdated

odious *(OH-dee-us), adjective*
Abhorrent, detestable

odyssey *(ODD-ih-see), noun*
A long journey entailing adventure and danger

officious *(uh-FISH-uss), adjective*
Overbearing, self-importantly rude in the exercise of authority

omniscient *(om-NISS-see-ent), adjective*
All-knowing

onerous *(ON-nur-uss), adjective*
Burdensome

opaque *(oh-PAYK), adjective*
Impenetrable to light; difficult to understand

opine *(oh-PINE), verb*
To hold or express an opinion

opus *(OPE-us), noun*
A work of art

ornate *(or-NATE), adjective*
Richly ornamented

oscillate *(OSS-ih-late), verb*
To go back and forth among opinions, beliefs, or plans

ostentatious *(oss-ten-TAY-shuss), adjective*
Showy of wealth or power

ostracize *(OSS-tra-size), verb*
To shun and exclude someone, especially for unconventional beliefs or practices

palpable *(PALP-a-bl), adjective*
Evident, obvious

pandemic *(pan-DEM-ik), adjective*
Widespread: used of a disease or other ill condition

pander *(PAN-der), verb and noun*
To appeal to the worst in people

papal *(PAY-pal), adjective*
Pertaining to the pope

paradigm *(PARE-a-dime), noun*
A model or theory that embraces a great number of particulars in an orderly way

paradox *(PAIR-a-doks), noun*
A seemingly self-contradictory statement or

condition that actually contains an elusive truth

paragon *(PARE-a-gon), noun*
A perfect embodiment and model of excellence

parameter *(pa-RAM-a-ter), noun*
A limit, boundary

parsimonious *(par-sih-MOAN-ee-uss), adjective*
Extremely spare and frugal

paucity *(PAW-si-tee), noun*
Smallness, lack of a sufficient number

pecuniary *(pe-KYOO-nee-air-ee), adjective*
Pertaining to money

pejorative *(pe-JORE-a-tiv), adjective*
Disparaging, speaking to make someone look inadequate

penultimate *(pen-UL-ti-met), adjective*
Next to last

peremptory *(pe-REMP-tuh-ree), adjective*
Speaking abruptly and not allowing for argument

perennial *(pe-REN-ee-ul), adjective*
Enduring, lasting through the years

perfunctory *(perr-FUNK-toh-ree), adjective*
Behaving indifferently, giving minimal attention to the demands of a task

periphery *(pe-RIFF-ih-ree), noun*
The area at the extreme of a boundary

perjure *(PURR-jer), verb*
To give false testimony

pernicious *(purr-NISH-uss), adjective*
Harmful

perspicacity *(per-spih-KASS-ih-tee), noun*
Insightfulness, perceptiveness

picayune *(pik-ay-YOON), adjective*
Trifling, of little account

platitude *(PLAT-ih-tude), noun*
A remark expressing commonplace beliefs and having no freshness or force

plethora *(PLETH-or-a), noun*
A vast oversupply

polarize *(PO-la-rize), verb*
To press opponents to irreconciliable positions

polemics *(pol-LEM-iks), noun*
Argument

posit *(PAHZ-it), verb*
To assert as a truth and as a beginning of discussion

pragmatic *(prag-MA-tik), adjective*
Pertaining to how ideas relate to experience

precocious *(pri-KOH-shuss), adjective*
Advanced beyond the normal level for the age of a child

presage *(PRESS-ij), verb*
To foretell, to give indication of the future

prevaricate *(pri-VARE-a-kate), verb*
To speak misleadingly for the purpose of avoiding the truth

pristine *(PRISS-teen), adjective*
In a wild natural state, unspoiled

propagate *(PROP-a-gate), verb*
To cause to multiply; to spread information in hope of persuading people

propinquity *(pro-PIN-kwih-tee), noun*
Nearness, blood kinship

prosaic *(pro-ZAY-ik), adjective*
Commonplace, workaday

proselytize *(PROSS-e-lih-tize), verb*
To attempt to convert others

protégé *(PRO-tay-zhay), noun*
A person protected, encouraged, or helped by a more secure or powerful benefactor

prototype *(PRO-toh-type), noun*
An original model to which later varieties can be traced

provocative *(pro-VOK-a-tive), adjective*
Stimulating, inviting argument

puerile *(PYOO-il), adjective*
Unduly immature in conduct

pugnacious *(pug-NAY-shuss), adjective*
Temperamentally inclined to verbal or physical combat

purported *(purr-POR-tid), adjective*
Reported, on insufficient evidence, to be so

putative *(PYOO-ta-tive), adjective*
Reputed, alleged

quagmire *(KWAG-mire), noun*
A marsh in which every step breaks the surface; an entanglement that offers no ready extrication

querulous *(KWER-uh-luss), adjective*
Complaining

ramification *(ram-ih-fih-KAY-shun), noun*
An eventual and possibly unintended consequence

rapport *(ra-PORE), noun*
A relationship in which the parties quickly understand and sympathize

rapprochement *(ra-prosh-MAWN), noun*
The bringing back together of quarreling parties

recant *(rih-KANT), verb*
To disavow

recumbent *(ri-KUM-bent), adjective*
Lying down

renege *(rih-NEG), verb*
To go back on a promise

replete *(rih-PLEET), adjective*
Filled, more than sufficiently supplied

replicate *(REP-li-kate), verb*
To make an exact likeness of an original

reprehensible *(rep-ri-HEN-sih-bl), adjective*
Abhorrent to morality

repugnance *(ri-PUG-nance), noun*
Disgust

requisite *(REK-wi-zit), adjective*
Necessary

resilience *(ri-ZIL-yence), noun*
The ability to rebound

reticent *(RET-ih-sent), adjective*
Reserved, shy

retroactive *(ret-ro-AK-tiv), adjective*
Effective back to a stated time

retrospect *(RET-roh-spekt), noun*
A looking back to the past

rubicon *(ROO-bih-kon), noun*
A point at which a decision to continue is irreversible

ruminate *(ROO-mih-nate), verb*
To ponder something closely and at length

rusticate *(RUSS-ti-kate), verb*
To return, at least momentarily, to rural life and behavior

salient *(SAY-lee-ent), adjective*
Standing out, relevant to the matter at hand

sanguine *(SAN-gwinn), adjective*
Confident, positive

savoir faire *(SAV-wahr FAIR), noun*
An easy ability to deal with social situations

scathing *(SKAY-thing), adjective*
Seethingly critical

schematic *(skee-MAT-ik), noun*
A diagram or scheme

scrutinize *(SKROOT-n-ize), verb*
To examine closely

semantics *(see-MAN-tiks), noun*
The study of how language relates to meaning

sententious *(sen-TEN-shuss), adjective*
Filled with brief, sharp comments

sequester *(si-KWES-ter), verb*
To set apart from outside influence

sine qua non *(SEE-nay kwa NOHN), noun*
An essential feature, "without which not"

sobriquet *(SO-bri-ket), noun*
A nickname

solace *(SOL-ess), noun*
Consolation

solecism *(SOL-ih-siz-um), noun*
A lapse in manners or other correctness

solicitous *(suh-LISS-ih-tuss), adjective*
Concerned in a careful way

sporadic *(spoh-RAD-ik), adjective*
Occurring occasionally or irregularly

spurious *(SPYOOR-ee-uss), adjective*
Inauthentic, falsely representative of something genuine

stereotype *(STAIR-ee-o-type), noun*
A simplified, ill-informed widely held image of a group

subjective *(sub-JEK-tiv), adjective*
Originating within the feelings of the individual

sublimate *(SUB-lih-mate), verb*
To transfer into a higher goal an energy originating in biological drives

superfluous *(soo-PER-floo-uss), adjective*
Exceeding what is needed

supersede *(soo-per-SEED), verb*
To supplant, replace

surfeit *(SUR-fit), noun*
Injurious excess

sycophant *(SIK-uh-fent), noun*
A self-seeking, groveling flatterer

symbiotic *(sim-bee-AH-tik), adjective*
Pertaining to two dissimilar organisms living in a mutually advantageous relationship

synopsis *(sih-NOP-sis), noun*
A brief summary, especially of a piece of fiction

taciturn *(TASS-ih-turn), adjective*
Withdrawn and brief of speech

tangible *(TAN-jih-bl), adjective*
Real, touchable

tantamount *(TAN-ta-mount), adjective*
Equivalent

temerity *(te-MARE-uh-tee), noun*
Rashness, boldness

tenacious *(te-NAY-shuss), adjective*
Stubborn in holding to an argument or a course of action

thespian *(THESS-pee-an), noun*
An actor

tirade *(TIE-raid), noun*
An outburst of bitter, angry speech

titular *(TICH-uh-lar), adjective*
By title only as opposed to wielding actual authority

transgression *(trans-GRESH-un), noun*
A violation of a rule

translucent *(tranz-LOO-sent), adjective*
Allowing some light to show through

trenchant *(TREN-chant), adjective*
A cutting, keen statement or argument

tryst *(trist), noun*
A prearranged meeting, especially if secret and between lovers

ubiquitous *(yoo-BIK-wi-tuss), adjective*
Seemingly everywhere

ultimatum *(ul-tih-MAY-tum), noun*
Final demand accompanied with an announcement of the action that will follow its rejection

undulate *(UN-dyoo-late), verb*
To move in a wavelike way

unilateral *(yoo-ni-LAT-er-el), adjective*
Undertaken independently of allies or opponents

usurp *(yoo-SURP), verb*
To take over power or office that belongs to someone else

usury *(YOO-sur-ee), noun*
Taking excessive interest on a loan

utopia *(yoo-TOE-pee-ah), noun*
Any theoretically conceived perfect society

vacillate *(VAS-ih-late), verb*
To waver between options

vacuous *(VAK-yoo-uss), adjective*
Empty of real ideas

vehement *(VEE-e-ment), adjective*
Strongly felt and energetically expressed

verbose *(ver-BOSE), adjective*
Wordy

verdant *(VUR-dnt), adjective*
Green

vernacular *(ver-NAK-yoo-lur), noun*
The daily language of a particular people

vicarious *(vi-KARE-ee-uss), adjective*
Lived at second hand through the experiences of others

vindicate *(VIN-dih-kate), verb*
To justify, especially in the face of possible criticism

visceral *(VISS-er-al), adjective*
Felt instinctively rather than reasoned

vitriolic *(vit-ree-OL-ik), adjective*
Scathing and viciously critical

vivacious *(vy-VAY-shuss), adjective*
High-spirited, sprightly

vociferous *(vo-SIF-er-uss), adjective*
Loud in announcement or insistence

volatile *(VOL-a-til), adjective*
Potentially unstable

wanton *(WON-tun), adjective*
Destructively reckless

watershed *(WAH-ter-shed), noun*
A swell in land that divides the flow of water; an event that changes the direction of the future

zealot *(ZEL-ut), noun*
A fervent, fanatical partisan

Appendix II

SPELLING

Misspelling, like poor punctuation, distracts the reader from the substance of what you are saying. Some poor spellers are people with inflated egos who regard mere mechanics as unworthy of the notice of real intellectuals. One best-selling style manual lists spelling at the rear of the book under "Spelling and Mechanics," implying that it is unimportant and unworthy of serious attention in college. Just memorize the correct spelling of these words you will otherwise spend a lifetime wondering how to spell and another lifetime looking up in dictionaries: *accommodate, across, all right, apparently, argument, benefited, calendar, changeable, develop, dilemma, embarrass, existence, familiar, forty, grammar, harass, maneuver, memento, Mississippi, misspell, occasionally, occurred, playwright, prejudice, privilege, professor, pronunciation, repetition, rhythm, separate, sergeant, sincerely, sophomore, succeed, tragedy, villain.*

Note three verbs in the present tense ending with "-eed": "proceed, exceed, succeed." Other words that sound similar, such as "recede" and "precede," end with "ede." And "i" comes before "e" except after "c," as in "receive." About a dozen exceptions exist when the vowel sound is like the "a" in "cage": among them are "neighbor," "freight," "eight," "weight" and "weigh." Note also *counterfeit, either, foreign, height, leisure, neither, seize, weird.*

Poor spellers may want to spend some time on this list of commonly misspelled words:

absence
absolutely
academic
accept
access
accessible
accidentally
accommodate
accompanying
accomplishment
according
accumulation
accurate
accuse
accustomed
ache
achievement
acknowledgment

acquaintance
across
activities
actually
address
adequate
adjacent
adolescent
advantage
advantageous
advertisement
advice
advisable
advise
adviser
affect
afraid
aggravate
aggressive
aisle
allot
allowance
almost
alphabet
already
although
amateur
ambitious
among

amount
analysis
analyze
announcement
annual
answer
antecedent
anticipation
antidote
antiseptic
anxiety
apartment
apology
apparatus
apparently
appearance
appendicitis
applied
appointment
appreciation
approach
appropriate
approval
approximately
arctic
argument
aroused
arrangement
article

ascend
assistance
association
athletic
attack
attendance
attitude
attractiveness
audience
author
authority
autobiography
autumn
auxiliary
available
awkward

bachelor
balloon
bargain
basically
beautiful
beauty
becoming
beggar
beginning
behavior
believing
beneficial
benefited
boundary
Britain
business

cafeteria
calendar
campaign
candidate
career
careless
category
celebrate
cemetery
century
changeable
characteristic
chauffeur
chocolate
choose
circumstance
coincidence
column
comfortably
commercial
commission
committee
communication
community

companies
comparatively
comparison
compatible
compel
competence
competition
completely
complexion
composition
comprehension
concede
conceivable
conceive
concentrated
concern
condemn
confidence
congratulations
connoisseur
conscience
conscientious
conscious
consensus
consequently
considerable
consistent
consolation
contemporary
contemptuous
continually
continuous
contribution
controlled
controversy
convenience
correspondence
councilor
counselor
countries
courageous
courtesy
criticism
criticize
cruel
curiosity
curriculum
customary
customer
cylinder

dangerous
dealt
deceive
decidedly
decision
defenseless
deficiency

deficient
definitely
definition
delinquent
dependent
depression
descendant
descent
diphtheria
disappear
disappoint
disastrous
disciple
discipline
disease
dissatisfied
dissipate
dominant
dormitories
drunkenness

ecstasy
edition
education
effect
efficiency
eighth
eighty
either
elementary
eligible
eliminate
eloquently
embarrass
eminent
emperor
emphasize
emptiness
encouragement
enemies
enormous
enough
enterprise
entertainment
enthusiasm
entirely
entrance
environment
equally
equipped
equivalent
especially
essential
eventually
evidently
exaggerating
exceed
excellent

exceptionally
excess
excitable
exercise
exhausted
exhibit
exhilarate
existence
expectation
expenses
experience
experiment
explanation
extravagant

facilities
faithfulness
fallacy
familiar
families
fantasy
fascinating
favorite
feasible
February
fictitious
finally
financially
financier

foreign
foreword
formally
formerly
forty
forward
fourteen
fourth
friendliness
fulfill

gaiety
gauge
genius
genuine
gorgeous
government
governor
grammar
grandeur
grievous
guarantee
guidance

handicapped
handkerchief
happening
happiness
harass

healthy
height
heroes
heroines
hindrance
hoping
hospitality
huge
humiliate
humorous
hurriedly
hygiene
hypocrisy
hypocrite

imaginary
immediately
immense
impassable
impossible
inadequate
inauguration
incidentally
incredible
indefinitely
independent
indictment
indispensable
individual
influential
ingenious
initiative
innocence
insistence
instructor
instrument
intellectual
interference
interpretation
interruption
intolerance
introductory
irrelevant
irresistible
irritable

jealousy
jewelry

kindergarten

labeled
laboratory
language
leisurely
license
lieutenant
likelihood

literature
livelihood
loneliness
lovable
luxuries

maintenance
maneuver
marriageable
meanness
meant
mechanics
millionaire
miniature
miscellaneous
mischief
mischievous
misspelled
mosquitoes
muscle
musician
mysterious

narrative
naturally
necessary
negative
Negro
Negroes
neighbor
neither
Niagara
niece
nineteen
ninety
ninth
noticeable

obstacle
occasionally
occurred
occurrence
omission
omitted
optimism
overwhelming

pamphlet
pandemonium
pantomime
parallel
paralyze
particularly
pastime
peaceable
peculiarities
penniless
perceive

permanent
permissible
perseverance
persistent
personnel
perspiration
phase
phenomenon
Philippines
physician
picnicking
plausible
playwright
pleasant
politician
possessions
practically
prairie
precedent
preceding
predominant
preferable
preference
preferred
prejudice
prescription
presence
prevalence
primitive

privilege
probably
proceed
professor
prominent
pronounce
pronunciation
propaganda
proprietor
pursue

questionnaire

receipt
receivable
recognize
recommend
reference
regrettable
relevant
relieve
religious
remembrance
reminisce
renowned
repentance
repetition
resources
responsibility

restaurant
reverent
rhythm
ridiculous
righteous
rivalry
roommate

sacrifice
sacrilegious
safety
sandwich
satirical
satisfaction
satisfied
Saturday
saucer
sausage
scarcity
scene
schedule
scheme
scholarship
scientific
secretary
seize
selection
sentence
separate

several
severely
shepherd
shriek
siege
similar
sincerely
situation
solution
sophomore
sovereignty
specialization
specifically
specimen
spectacle
speech
sponsor
stenographer
straighten
strength
strenuous
stubborn
studying
subscription
substantiate
substitute
subtle
succeeding
suddenness

sufficient
summarize
superintendent
supersede
supervisor
suppress
surprise
surrounded
susceptible
suspense
suspicious
swimming
syllable
symbol
symmetrical
synonymous

tactfulness
technical
technique
temperament
temperate
temporarily
tenant
tendency
tenement
theories
therefore
thirtieth
thirty
thoroughly
thought
thousand
together
tomorrow
tradition
tragedy
transferred
transportation
tremendous
trespass
truly
Tuesday
twelfth
twentieth
typical
tyranny

unanimous
unbelievable
uncivilized
unconscious
uncontrollable
undesirable
undoubtedly
uneasiness
unforgettable
universities

unmanageable
unnecessary
until
unusual
usually

vacuum
valleys
valuable
varieties
various
vaudeville
vegetable
vengeance
ventilate
verbatim
vernacular
versatile
veteran
vicinity
victim
villain
vinegar
virtuous
visible
vitamin
volume

waive
warranted
wealthiest
weather
Wednesday
weird
wholly
wintry
withholding
wrench
writing
written

yacht
Yankee
yield

zealot
zenith
zero

ACKNOWLEDGMENTS

Brandywine Press would like to thank John McClymer, who wrote the original version of Succeeding in History Courses; Tom West, who went over and over the entire manuscript; Laura Mentz, who assisted in the production of the book; David Burner, who provides the first person voice in the opening section; Susan Senter of Brandywine's proofreading staff; and Mel Rosenthal, a twenty-five year veteran of Alfred A. Knopf's copyediting department. All of the contributors would be grateful to receive any criticisms c/o Brandywine Press, 158 Triple Oak Lane, St. James, NY 11780 or by phone at 1-800-345-1776.